Benjamin Hathaway

Art-Life

And Other Poems

Benjamin Hathaway

Art-Life
And Other Poems

ISBN/EAN: 9783744711104

Printed in Europe, USA, Canada, Australia, Japan

Cover: Foto ©Thomas Meinert / pixelio.de

More available books at **www.hansebooks.com**

AND OTHER POEMS

BY

BENJAMIN HATHAWAY.

" Laurel crowns cleave to deserts,
And power to him who power exerts.
Hast not thy share? On winged feet,
Lo! it rushes thee to meet;
And all that Nature made thy own,
Floating in air or pent in stone,
Will rive the hills and swim the sea,
And, like thy shadow, follow thee."
—Ralph Waldo Emerson.

SECOND THOUSAND, REVISED.

CHICAGO:
S. C. GRIGGS & COMPANY.
1878.

All hearts the Poet fires are his :
The subtle link of mind to mind —
The link we do not forge and bind,
    Most precious is ; —
We mine — not make — the golden ore,
And love, like fabled fairy store,
Divided, is not less but more, ·
    And true love hath no jealousies.

PRESS OF DONNELLEY, LOYD & CO., CHICAGO.

TO MY MOTHER.

Thou type of noblest Womanhood!
Thou who in manhood's evil day,
As by the couch of infancy,
       Still faithful stood;
Unfaltering, and with purpose strong,
Rebuking all the hosts of wrong,
With "Lore is more than gift of song,"
       And "Virtue is the highest good."

Oh would these wildwood flowers for thee
Were robed in Beauty's charm and bloom,
Made rich with every rare perfume
       Of Poesy;
With every grace of heart and mind,
With Woman in all reverence shrined;
In part repaying so in kind
       A debt as boundless as the sea.

CONTENTS.

ART-LIFE.

I looked on Genius when his face shone grand
  With fire of inspiration; when up-caught
  And borne afar—a being fairer wrought
    And nobler planned,
  Of purer clay, by finer instinct taught
To fashion Beauty with a cunning hand—
  To build incarnate an undying Thought.

And I so poor—the partial Fates deny
  His larger gift—did murmur and repine;
  Yet mine no less a heritage divine—
    As pure and high;
  All are true heirs of the Immortal Nine!
I too have wealth that gold can never buy:
  I love—and lo! all that was his is mine.

ART-LIFE.

WHAT prophet wide with trumpet tongue is teaching
   The chainèd world its thought of Liberty,
Till loving hearts go out in meek beseeching
   And wild unbosomed longing to be free?
What stranger truth is new evangel preaching
     Of Life to be?

Divinest Art! thou heaven of our aspiring,
   Wherein our being is in doing blest,
And duty is at one with our desiring —
   The radiant goal of all earth's empty quest;
The sternest toiling evermore untiring —
     The sweetest rest!

O joy supreme! labor unvexed of wages!
   The equipoise of Good that all things wait;
Care that all care, pain that all pain assuages;
   Bonds that are free — the brotherhood of Fate;
The Love unpledged that lives through all the ages
     Inviolate.

Who shall the Life so beautiful unseal us —
    The life whose labor is a work of bliss?
When shall our doing of our doing heal us?
    Our toiling rest us of our weariness?
Thou God within us, to ourselves reveal us
            In perfectness!

A desert-way we wander unavailing;
    Anear the babbling brook we fainting lie,
Or on and on — forevermore bewailing
    Each fading bright oasis seeming nigh:
Lead us by living waters never failing,
            Oh, else we die!

With maniac hands, each nobler purpose foiling,
    We strive to do, yet know not how or why;
We come not to our own in all our toiling,
    We live a falsehood till we love the lie;
And, strangers to ourselves, our gifts despoiling,
            We live and die.

Might bread alone appease this deathless yearning,
    For bread alone to toil were meet and fit;
But oh, we feel, however dimly burning
    Within the soul the fire celestial lit,
If Love is not the wages of our earning
            What profits it?

Ungenial toil, our meaner wants supplying,
  Our better life for this its birthright sells;
In all our doing we are only dying
  With quenchless thirsting for Art's living wells:
Give us the labor and the self-denying,
      Genius impels!

Genius, that is of Virtue the fair flowering —
  All noble aspirations, true and brave;
The deathless love with life immortal dowering
  Alike the pencilled dream, the poet's stave,
The sculptured bust, the chiselled column towering
      To architrave.

All-conquering Genius! where is now thy dwelling?
  In what fair clime is reared Minerva's home?
Whose proudest fanes Time's rudest hand is felling:
  Immortal Athens' beauty-sculptured dome;
Thy Coliseum, of Art's triumph telling,
      Imperial Rome!

Where lives the soul — in what fair incarnation —
  That woke of old the desert-city's smile?
Palmyra, peerless in thy devastation!
  And hundred-gated Thebes — stupendous pile,
Girding the waste in awful desolation
      By sacred Nile!

Oh, still meseems more vital breath distilling
  From crumbling dome where alien footstep treads;
A haughty glance of nobler being dwelling
  In stern repose of Ammon's stony lids —
Of morning Memnon, glory-smitten, thrilling
      The Pyramids!

Beneath thy dust what hoary gods are sleeping —
  Deathless heroes, drunken on lotus balm!
Around whose couch are nameless sphinxes keeping
  Their hallowed watches, robed in sullen calm;
By many a long-forgotten shrine is weeping
      The desert palm.

Oh, day by day, with an intenser yearning,
  How do we turn with still expectant eyes
To greet thy rising day more fair returning,
  Divinest Art! than lit thy morning rise
On Grecian hills, or sunset-halo burning
      Italia's skies!

Perchance our life in light so sweetly tender
  Has some reflected grandeur faintly caught;
To thee these weaker years still turn with wonder.
  Sublimer age! with inspiration fraught,
When Pericles outrayed immortal splendor,
      And Phidias wrought.

Alas! how prone the weary years are fleeing
　In lust of gold, or fame's unquiet quest;
With heart and hand in endless disagreeing
　O'er miscalled duties — while in every breast
Lives the monition of more beauteous being,
　　　In vague unrest.

The youth glad hears his better genius calling,
　Like far-off murmur of unquiet seas;
In vain he waits more happy hours befalling —
　Time heartless speeds apace, life's morning flees;
Age seals his fiery lip — some world-enthralling
　　　Demosthenes.

And maiden heart, in rarest dream elysian,
　Would thrill all being with a love-refrain;
But Nature's need, and endless improvision
　Of household care, or oft maternal pain,
Swift breaks the spell of each too ardent vision
　　　And dreaming vain.

How many a soul by world of sorrow shaded,
　Deep in whose wells the gems of Genius shine —
How many a hand with weary task o'erladed,
　But digs the soil or delves the darkened mine —
That could have wrought, by kindlier fortune aided,
　　　A work divine!

And who may say, whom more of strength embolden
　　Or chance from meaner care some respite win,
The happier few — if throned in region golden
　　Of radiant Art, afar from strife and din,
What forms transcendent, by oblivion holden,
　　　　　There might have been?

Oh, ever on untrodden walks ascending
　　To drink from Inspiration's storied well,
On heights of song in loftier glory bending.
　　Free of the boundless universe to dwell!
Like olden Bard, a life serenely lending
　　　　　To Beauty's spell!

To tread with wingèd feet and heart imperial
　　The hills of morn, with sparry splendors rife;
A cloudless realm of loving light aërial,
　　Unwrecked of wrong, ungloomed of pain and strife:
High crowned and glorious in a world ethereal—
　　　　　Life's dream of Life!

Alas! deep thirsting for the wave enchanted
　　No summer prime unseals those limpid springs:
Far gazing on the mountain way undaunted,
　　And glad to soar above all meaner things,
The longing spirit lags, though vision-haunted,
　　　　　On wearied wings.

And prone are thousands by the wayside lying;
   Crushed are their aspirations, but not dead;
For some high Art, diviner being, sighing —
   For free, true life, unsoiled of want and dread;
Toiling and toiling — a vain self-denying
      For daily bread.

With longings vain, and strivings all unaided,
   No longer beaconed by Hope's lustrous light,
In vain they mourn life's fair ideal faded;
   Their morning sun at noon is set in night;
In vain they seek the doing undegraded —
      A life-delight.

Yet evermore new aspirations springing
   Like summer flowers, our winter paths adorn;
And, wearing late, the glooming night is bringing
   Anon the better prophecy of morn;
Though still we wait, through ages darkly winging
      An Æon born —

When Life shall flow like some wide-rolling river,
   A far, free, shining course serenely run;
To brighten, deepen, broaden on forever,
   The days of its high destiny begun;
When Love and Labor nevermore shall sever —
      Their being one.

We are the lights on Life's mysterious dial,
  The radiant stops on Love's celestial horn;
High Heaven's orchestra on untutored trial,
  With harps discordant, dolorous, and forlorn;
Or waiting, hushed, like Egypt's stony viol,
      The flush of morn.

O Life of Art! Thou life serene and holy —
  Thou God-ordainèd balm for every woe!
Upwing thy sovereign day that lightens slowly;
  Unchain each suffering soul that would be true;
Whate'er our part, if proud it be or lowly,
      Give us to do!

Oh, once again with medicine and healing
  Into our hearts on rhythmic measures float;
A higher life in nobleness unsealing,
  Unveiling near Love's ancient heaven remote:
For every evil of our flesh revealing
      The antidote.

As mountain pine, in rugged grandeur growing,
  Finds Nature's fullness in that bleak abode,
Or lowly blooms, its inner life outshowing.
  The humblest flower that decks the meadow sod:
So finds the soul in Art's diviner doing
      Its home in God.

There limpid springs the Fount of Youth eternal,
   That many a league our weary feet beguiles;
There lie Hesperian fields serene and vernal,
   Whose magic shore from far receding smiles;
Anchored in thee, the evergreen, supernal
     Enchanted Isles.

Therein alone we drink Life's blest oblation;
   There lives the Real our Ideal brings;
Therein we roam — an endless recreation —
   Untrodden paths that lie by living springs;
Therein is giving to our aspiration
     Unfettered wings.

Thou final Good! the theme of wisest sages;
   Beginning, end, and goal of Liberty;
The choral hymn that echoes down the ages,
   The inspiration of all prophecy,
The golden days all Poet's song presages —
     The TIME TO BE!

.

Our feeble hands in thee alone are mighty,
   In thee our triumph in o'ermastering strife;
We turn to thee, as to yon heavens nightly,
   Far seeming ever with new glories rife;
For Art-Love only is the Elixir-Vitæ —
     The LIFE OF LIFE!

2

MISSISSIPPI.

If aught can lift the Soul to nobler mood —
From thought and feeling prone,
From passion's baser sway, life disenthrall —
Full on the heights enthrone, —
It is to roam the rerdured solitude,
Alone, yet not alone;
To hark the voices from the silence call,
Dear as each household tone;
To feel, with Nature's ampler life imbued,
Free as the free winds blown,
The heart full pulsing with the heart of all —
One with the Great Unknown.

MISSISSIPPI.

ALL HAIL! thou mighty stretch of inland sea,
　Now for the first unto my sight outlying!
No faintly-canvassed imagery of thee.
But in thy glory and thy majesty
　Murmuring immortal harmonies, outvying
　The troubled ocean in its fitful sighing —
　　The tide-disturbing sea.

Oft have I wandered in a visioned dream
　Through radiant summer lands of memories olden;
Where rock and hill and vale and wood and stream
Far glanced and brightened to the kindling beam
　Of fairer, sunnier climes, serene and golden;
　While heart and thought in mystic band were holden
　　In one long radiant dream.

But peerless thy sublimity of scene:
 Looming immense, in stern wild grandeur sleeping,
Thy hills, far glimmering in the noontide sheen.
The headlong rush of eddying floods between
 Wave - warding cliffs, thy shores high overleaping,
 With many a legend strange in their dim keeping,
  Surpass each dream - born scene.

Far as the eye can trace I see thy might
 Of hurrying waters in their seaward flashing;
While cleaving yonder deeps of crystal light
Ledge high on ledge uprears a dizzy height,
 Majestic frowning on thy wayward dashing,
 Chafing the echoing shores with ceaseless lashing
  And still unwearied might.

Thy voiceful murmur hath a cadence deep,
 That Echo answers from her craggy dwelling;
Waked are thy billows from their icy sleep,
And madly surging as they rush and leap
 O'er all the embosomed valley wildly welling;
 Or fearful and resistless onward - swelling .
  Unto the waiting deep.

Yet thine the music of the mountain springs —
   The swelling song of myriad rillets blending;
Each tiny fount its rippling treasure brings,
That far amid the Alleghanies sings;
   While in the sunset - land, their tribute lending,
   Are serried, snow - capped, bleak Sierras, sending
      Their glad eternal springs.

And it were joy their shining track to trace
   Through thousand green savannas to their sources;
Fair fenceless fields in Nature's wildest grace
Thy countless streams meandering interlace;
   Still hastening, murmuring, dallying in their courses,
   Through many a wild where Art's despoiling forces
      Have left no darkening trace.

Charmed with the music of thy lullaby
   So softly crooning to the Hesper - even,
Forgot the anguish of each sundered tie,
The wrongs forgotten of the years gone by,
   The harsher world forgotten and forgiven —
   How might I hear the seraph - song of Heaven
      In thy soft lullaby!

Blest with some friend of sympathizing breast,
  Though prone to err, yet loving and forgiving.
And taught of sorrow that the sweetest rest,
The fullest blessing, is in making blest;
  That truest balm for pain is pain - relieving;
  Whose thought upreaches to the ever - living
      All - sympathizing breast, —

How sweet to dwell apart from care and strife,   '
  By grove and stream with inspiration teeming;
To hail each day with some new rapture rife.
To taste the true sublimity of life
  In some fair sylvan haunt of Eden - seeming.
  More beauteous than charms the poet's dreaming.
      Unvexed with care and strife:

Where no rude sound disturbs the tranquil dream,
  The sacred calm on earth and azure lying;
Where mellowed murmurs of each laughing stream
That glances wanton in the glittering beam,
  The wood - bowers wakened to a soft replying,
  Or hushed as listening to thy farewell sighing —
      All weave enchanted dream.

There, where the gardens of the desert shine,
The housewife bee her busy craft is plying,
Industrious hoarding till the day's decline
From blushing wood - rose and sweet eglantine
    The luscious stores, her winter wants supplying:
Nor rests from toil till Autumn pale is sighing,
        And dimmed each floweret's shine.

There through the quiet of the summer days
    Rises the mound, the cunning gopher's mining;
There undisturbed the tameless bison strays,
The wary elk and moose securely graze —
    Are lazily on mossy bank reclining;
While the long hours are bright with sun and shining
        And breath of summer days.

Unmeasured leagues, where thy glad fountains rise,
    The Red Man rears his rude bark - covered dwelling;
His simple wants the wonted chase supplies;
Nor taught to miss what partial Fate denies,
    His heart elate with warrior pride is swelling,
Unmindful of the prophet - voices telling
        Of darker days' uprise.

3

There the young hunter with a boldness rare
  Roams the deep forest as the day is whiling.
To trail the panther to his lonely lair
Or thread the mazes of the wily bear —
  · Brave deeds alone his every thought beguiling.
  Such as may win the bright eyes' kindliest smiling
    Of forest - maiden rare.

There too, as deepens the departing day,
  The dark - eyed daughter of the desert, stealing
From the home - wigwam silently away,
Unchidden wanders in the twilight ray
  To list confiding unto Love's revealing;
  While blissful promise, to her sight unsealing.
    Floods many a coming day.

And who shall say if yet her lowly life.
  So seeming shut in want and degradation,
Mid forest wilds, mid scenes of warrior - strife,
Through all its changeful years of maid and wife
  Finds not alone in love the compensation
  Of every loss: O heavenly constellation.
    Set in the lowliest life!
      *   *   *

And thou: what wondrous voices from the Past
Do babble to us in thy waves' deploring
Of mightiest secrets in oblivion cast!
Who shall unseal them from the slumbering vast?
  Re-tune thy lyre, some olden strain outpouring,
  The lore of long-departed days restoring,
    Thou Spirit of the Past!

Weave us some Idyl of the Ages flown!
· Help thou our reason in its weak divining,
To read the record of the years unknown!
The site of ancient empires overthrown,
  The crumbled wall the forest dimly lining,
  Where bows the cypress to the ivy's twining,
    Tell of the ages flown.

These, the memorials of the days of yore,
  Reveal the Present to the Past related:
A race, a people, that are now no more,
Here reared proud temples on thy lonely shore —
  Of strange and unremembered art created,
  To long-forgotten worship consecrated
    In the far days of yore. [1]

For thou hast looked on minaret and dome—
  On thronging cities that the earth is hiding:
Whose days were numbered ere the infant Rome
Had wrought the grandeur of each palace home;
  Some senior Carthage in her glory priding.
  Some old imperial Thebes—though unabiding
    Arch, column, wall, and dome.

Some elder Athens of the Astalan,
  Rites, altars, fanes, all that the worship aided
Of Isis, Buddha, or an older than
These hoary gods,—old as the life of Man;
  Some ancient Tyre, august and undegraded.
  By the destroying hand of Time invaded.—
    Pride of the Astalan. [2]

Some rare Damascus of the elder world,
  Prouder than her the Syrian gardens shading;
Nineveh, on thy fairer shores impearled;
Some Babylon from her foundations hurled,
  Ere thine, Euphrates, saw her glory fading;
  Silently teaching—history upbraiding—
    Thine is the elder world.

What time the bison by the gleaming maize,
　Or o'er the furrowed glebe the share constraining.
Through all the loitering sultry summer days,
Where now untamed his thousand fellows graze.
　Bent his strong shagged shoulder uncomplaining.
　The netted muzzle him alone restraining
　　From the fair-gleaming maize.

Where vale and hill and wide-expanding plain
　And grassy field, unshorn. uncultured lying.
To beauty quickened by the sun and rain.
Waved golden billowed with the ripened grain;
　While busy swains, the frugal sickle plying.
　With cheerful song to cheerful song replying.
　　Enchanted all the plain.

When as the day wore tranquil to its close.
　The hour of labor with the daylight ending,
From sylvan homes of undisturbed repose
The vesper hymn in thankfulness arose
　From loving hearts in one communion blending:
　A truthful life of true affection lending
　　Light to its final close.

Long peaceful years in peasant-labor led,
  No bloody deeds its simple joys degrading;
A guileless race in rural freedom bred.
Unskilled in arts that fill the earth with dread.
  Its pleasant places with a fearful shading:
  No thirst for gain or selfish aim invading
    The simple life they led.

All, all have vanished from the earth away.
  And none are left their tragic end declaring:
If swiftly blotted from the face of day,
Of war, of famine, pestilence the prey,
  If haply wrought to deeds of fearless daring
  They nobly bled, unconquered, undespairing,
    Till life had ebbed away.

The fierce and warlike Hunter-tribes arose—
  The wandering lost of Israel's bewailing:
If thickly compassed with barbaric foes,
To warrior arm must warrior arm oppose;
  The earth-built barriers were unavailing:
  No free-born race survives, its freedom failing,
    Where its free altars rose.

And long unnumbered centuries have flown;
  Arch, dome, and wall have yielded to their grading:
Where on the plain the smiling cities shone
A dense and rugged wilderness has grown;
  The altar-mound the ancient oak is shading;
  Each lingering trace is darkly dim and fading.
    And soon shall all be flown.
        *   *   *

But oh, what vision of the Golden Year,
  As from their trance thy slumbering billows started!
To see across the solitudes austere
Adventurous bark thy regal empire near —
  A stalwart band, rude-girt yet fearless-hearted;
  The kindling dawn the misty night-gloom parted —
    Dawn of the Golden Year:

.

When he, the knight with snowy locks, but still
  His fiery heart with youthful ardor burning.
Sought on thy Gulf's far shores the mystic rill.
The legend-promised Fount whose springs distil
  Perpetual Youth, its vernal bloom returning:
  He came — he went — with disappointment yearning.
    His white locks whiter·still. [3]

And he, grim seeker, further on — his quest
  The Fount of Youth, of Eldorado dreaming,
Glad hailed thee, sinking on thy banks to rest:
Though life was ebbing in his aged breast,
  Full with exultant joy his great heart teeming —
" Behold, more rich than treasured Ophir gleaming,
    The objects of our quest!" *

As though transported to thy farthest shore,
  In rarer light, his mortal vision failing,
He gazed in wonder on each hidden store:
On wealth immeasured of the glittering ore,
  These later years to outer sight unveiling:
And heard the hosts of tramping miners trailing
    To-day thy farthest shore.

But he too sought the hidden spot in vain;
  His comrades left him to thy billows' caring;
Then mournful turning from that task of pain,
With thoughts that whispered of their native Spain,
  Of dark eyes weeping, of Love's long despairing,
  Went sorrowing on; but saddened memories bearing
    Of that wild vision vain.

Wild vision vain?—that was prophetic dream:
  The meaner type of man's prophetic yearning;
And here by thee, De Soto's mighty stream,
Shall yet the long-sought Eldorado gleam;
  Where all shall find, the Golden Days returning.
  The truest wealth; the deeper import learning
    Of that wild fabled dream.

Through radiant vistas of the coming time
  I see the glories of the Future's bringing,
Fair as the promise of Creation's prime;
The prophet voice of poet-seer sublime
  Still cheers our aspirations lowly springing:
  The fleeing years are through swift circles winging
    Unto the Better Time:

When gentle deeds shall bless an ampler day;
  Whose rising beam, a rayless night succeeding.
Flushes with rosy dawn the twilight gray;
When life shall kindle with serener ray,
  And Art and Science, in their upward leading.
  And Genius, on her starry pathway speeding.
    Shall bless the risen day.

4

Though thrice a hundred leagues of Silent Land —
Or but thy voice the solitudes beguiling —
Stretch far away to where sublimely stand
The cloud-girt snow-capped mountains lone and grand.
   Erelong in noontide beam of Freedom smiling
   Shall cities of a free-born nation's piling
      Fill all the Silent Land.

On all is change—the mystic change of life.
   The breath divine forever all things freeing;
The world is girded for its progress-strife:
The lonely desert with its voice is rife—
   The solitary place afar is fleeing;
   The Form is changeful, as the Soul of Being
      Ascends to higher life.

Though changing, still unchanged forevermore
   In thy vast cycles, boundless and unending,
Still onward do thy billows ceaseless pour,
While empires bloom and fade along thy shore,
   Till nobler dust with meaner dust is blending;
   From age to age thy anthem-song ascending
      Rings out forevermore.

NOTES.

1. " This ancient race seems to have occupied nearly the whole basin of
the Mississippi and its tributaries, with the fertile plains along the Gulf, and
their settlements were continued across the Rio Grande into Mexico."

Baldwin's Ancient America, p. 32.

2. " The people inhabiting the Vale of Mexico at the time the Spaniards
overrun that country, were called Astecks — having come from the North,
from a country they called Astalan ; literally, a country of much water."

See *Humboldt's Researches in South America*.

3. Juan Ponce de Leon. In the 16th century, this enthusiastic adventurer
visited a portion of the continent lying on the Gulf, while in command of
an expedition fitted out by himself, for discovering the Fountain of Youth,
which was thought by the natives of Porto Rico to exist in one of the Lucayo
Isles. Its virtues were such that all who bathed in its waters would be
restored to the bloom of youth.

See *Robertson's History of America*.

4. Hernando De Soto. " Mournfully depositing the body of their beloved
commander, wrapped in his mantle, in the trunk of an evergreen Oak, hol-
lowed out for that purpose, they reverently lowered it at midnight beneath
the waters of that magnificent river he had been the first to discover."

Discovery of the Mississippi.

VOICES FROM NATURE.

As child bewildered in the thronging mart,
  We look on Nature as a pageant grand,
    But only as the pageant of an hour;
      Nor see that all—tree, shrub, and forest flower,
  June roses rare, by Summer breezes fanned,—
Bloom evermore in gardens of the heart.

The woodland bird that sings, surpassing art,
  The insect life that thrills the twilight hour,
    The mountains vast, the tide-led seas that roll
      From Arctic Pole unto Antarctic Pole,
  Are all a portion of the Spirit's dower—
Are all of the Immortal Soul a part.

SNOW-BIRD.

O ARCTIC rover bold!
When forth in fierce array,
Resistless borne from farthest Labrador,
With tyrant sway
The icy squadrons pour —
Rage wide o'er wood and wold,
What never-dying love thy bosom warms!
What dauntless heart thy puny wings enfold,
To breast the wintry storms —
Thou scorner of the cold!

I see thee come and go
In thy swift eager flight,
Piercing the keen cold air with sudden wing
Of quick delight —
A bright ethereal thing;
While, like the flitting show
Of poet thoughts that scarce embodied are,
A thousand storm-led kindred pinions glow,
Upswirled and blown afar —
A cloud of drifting snow.

Are all alike to thee
The storm and sunshine? — are
The ever-changeful seasons as they go
Forever fair?
Is in thy breast the glow
Of suns we may not see —
Lighting thy way so airily, to wed
Joys of the past to joy and mystery
Of realms thy wings shall thread,
Journeying fleet and free?

Nor toil is thine, nor care:
For thee the wayside weeds
And frosted hedge-row yield an ample store
Of ripened seeds;
And every land and shore
Where thy free pinions bear,
Is all thine own; in Nature's mother-heart
Is thine abode; in all the homeless air
Domesticate thou art:
Thy home is everywhere.

They tell us, far remote
In woodland mountain air,
Amid Katahdin's shadow-haunted glooms,
When June hours fair
Are gay with summer blooms,

Thine is a minstrel throat
That charms with song the love - delighted days.
Thrilling the silence of each cave and grot:
Wake, of remembered lays.
One joy - inspiring note!

Oh, but to enter in
Thy fairer world! to see,
We know not what — though knowing all is fair,
Whatever be,
As the transcendent air
Of heaven to souls that win
Release from mortal ills: no tired brain
O'er unsolved mysteries, no battle - din.
No tears, no loved in vain,
No loss, no might - have - been.

What deeper sight is thine,
With what a soul possessed,
Thou pretty pinch of clay — thou sturdy, bold
Evangelist,
Preacher of gospel old!
Had I the subtle, fine
Ethereal blood that thrills thy radiant dust —
Had such unstudied art this harp of mine,
Thy simple love and trust
All human hearts should shrine.

Ah me! if cognizant
Of all thy little needs
Is One, with tender breast to pity stirred,
Who loves and feeds
Even thee, my lowly bird,
That Winter cannot daunt:
An Eye that sees, a Hand that holds and guides
Thy devious flight across a continent,
And evermore provides,
Forecasting every want: —

Is it less provident
Of thee — the care divine?
Less worthy thou of the benignant heed,
O heart of mine,
In this thy human need?
Love's shining battlement
Leans evermore above Time's clouded strand:
See in all loss, all wrong, all accident,
A loving Father's hand,
And seeing, be content.

PEBBLES.

ALONG the sea lies Summer's purple sheen;
  The drowsy waves low lapse, with fond caress,
On amber sands; in fading light serene.
      All purposeless
I wander where wide leagues of vernal green
    And blue seas loving kiss.

Beneath my feet uncounted pebbles gride,
  Strewn with unstinted hand on all the shore;
Some mighty Titan, rising from the tide,
      Them hither bore
Up from earth's hidden workshop caverns wide —
    Up from her granite floor.

Sandstone and flint from many a rocky trave,
  Chips from the walls of dark Devonian keeps;
All glomerates from caves where Ocean's wave
      Untroubled sleeps;
Schist, schale, and limestone, from the flags that pave
  . The old Silurian deeps.

Hornblende and mica from the tidal locks
　　Down to whose depths no plummet line may go;
Porphyry and feldspar from earth's primal rocks
　　　　Here pale and glow:
Gneiss and basalt from the unquarried blocks
　　Of her foundations low.

Quartz, trap, and slate, from many a dyke and turn
　　Deep in the cosmic mines; unsoiled of fame,
Agate and jasper from each billowy urn
　　　　With rocks that came
Up from the vaults where ever seethe and burn
　　Red seas of quenchless flame.

God's alphabet, could we interpret it
　　Aright, are ye; ye are—entraced as if
In monograph, in bits of mountain grit
　　　　And rocky cliff—
Creation's book, in mystic cypher writ,
　　In Nature's hieroglyph.

Could we but read its vast similitudes,
　　The wisdom of its ancient pages con,
Life's morning hymn through all its interludes
　　　　Still sounding on,
How might we hear—see, where but darkness broods,
　　Light of a higher sun!

To mighty secrets ye do hold the key;
   Could ye but tell by what convulsions torn,
All ye have seen of change while ages flee
      And worlds are born,
Here chafed and washed by the incessant sea,
   To forms of beauty worn.

Oh for the gift, the lore to understand!
   Yet what am I? — through elemental strife
Upborne as ye — up from what hidden land
      With wonder rife?
A pebble. thrown upon life's stormy strand,
   Broke from the Prime of Life.

But ye are mute, howbeit, mute to me;
   Though all too long I vain your silence mourn.
Hear but the homeless moaning of the sea
      On shores forlorn,
Or vaguely dream of beauty yet to be
   In some untravelled bourn:

Enough to know. around me not in vain
   The troubled tides of Being darkly press:
Grief, care. want, hope deferred, love's ache and strain,
      The passions' stress:
So grows the soul immortal. wrought through pain
   Into all comeliness.

FOREST HAUNTS.

Ye olden oaks, deep clad in greenness vernal,
　With Summer's sunlight on your rugged brows,
Methinks I hear the voice of the Eternal
　Go out amid the swaying of your boughs.

Oh, not the mythic fear-inspiring Monarch
　That but with dread our doubting thoughts invest.
But He who bears above Wrong's thronèd Anarch
　Earth's sorrowing children on his loving breast.

And oft unto your solemn shades retiring
　Of temple, altar, shrine, my heart to him
Has poured the burden of its high aspiring
　In measured cadence through your cloisters dim.

As wayward child, touched by some anguished arrow
　From the full quiver of the coming years,
On mother's breast unbosoms wild its sorrow,
　While loving kisses dry the brimming tears;

So turn I. yearning for your dear caressing;
World - worn and weary do I come again
To win some measure of maternal blessing,
If but a brief forgetfulness of pain.

From Life's fierce conflict, from its toil unending
Awhile to rest me where no care intrudes,
And feel my soul in quickened pulses blending
With kindred souls that dwell in solitudes;

To lowly listen to the mystic voices
That through your boundless sanctuaries ring,
And feel, while Nature in her heart rejoices,
Some thrill of rapture in my own upspring.

The mossy bank wears meek a smile of blessing;
There lives a gladness in each floral bell,
A spirit-healing in the mild caressing
Of balmy zephyrs in the woodland dell.

And hark! a thousand tiny throats are winging
Joy's silvery songs amid the murmuring trees;
O happy choir! a choral anthem singing —
The blended music of the birds and bees.

These shall restore me to the pure and tender
  Of feelings sullied in embittered strife;
Some faint ray kindle of Hope's morning splendor,
  That shed a halo on each dream of life.

O gentle Spirit that afar is hiding
  In unfrequented wilds of wood and glen,
Couldst thou as in these tranquil haunts abiding
  Dwell in the homes and in the hearts of men,

I had not need to medicine this longing
  With calm and quiet in your green retreat:
Life's stony paths, with weary pilgrims thronging,
  Were fair and flowery to these bleeding feet.

CHICKADEE.

WHAT time the Oriole
Through verdured haunts by spicy breezes fanned
Pours his full soul,
Far off in tropic land,
In wildest minstrelsy, —
If not so glad and gay,
Here in December woods, as blithe and free,
I hear thy gleeful note the livelong day —
My Chickadee!

Is all this storm and gloam
Of Winter vain to chill thy heart of song?
Dost never roam
With the proud minstrel throng
To climes beyond the sea?
What secret dost thou hold?
Is in thy breast the wondrous alchemy,
Transmuting all these leaden skies to gold —
My Chickadee?

Oh, for the subtle art
To share thy life, unsoiled of strife and din;
   A life apart
We may not enter in —
     A realm of mystery!
   Yet, though we may not cross
Its hidden bound, we feel it cannot be
  A weary world of ill and pain and loss —
     My Chickadee!

   Within thine eye so bright
No shadow lies of care or want or dread;
   There shines a light
More than of summers dead
     Or summers yet to be:
   Like to the morning glow
On Eden hills serene;— say, canst thou see
  The fairer world behind this fading show —
     My Chickadee?

   Is thine the vision rare
To pierce the gloom that hides the heavenly bourn
   Where all is fair?
The hidden land we mourn
     Unsorrowed dost thou see?

Then at thy cheerful stave
I marvel not, indeed, nor how it be
    Thy tiny breast can bear a heart so brave —
        My Chickadee!

    Oh, what a joyous song
Above this gloom and darkness would I pour —
    How free and strong
This weary heart would soar,
      That Morning Land to see!
Where blight and storm and frost
And grief and pain and parting may not be;
    Where glorified do wait our loved and lost —
        My Chickadee!

    Sole friend the Summer hides
That does not flee when summer hours are fled;
    That still abides
When vernal blooms are dead
      O'er hill and vale and lea;
Oh, when the roundelays
Of rarer throats are hushed, still keep for me
    Some breath of song to cheer life's darker days —
        My Chickadee!

WHIPPOORWILL.

O LONELY Night-bird from across the main,
    That oft hath soothed me with a plaintive hymn!
Once more the music of thy sad refrain
    Wakes the deep cloisters of the greenwood dim;
From out the twilight's still repose I hear
    Lorn Echo answering to thy sober song,—
A note, though mournful, to my heart more dear
    Than gayer numbers of the minstrel throng.

Oft when the piping of thy ceaseless plaint
    Rings out at even from the dusky wild,
Outsoaring all, time, tears, and sorrow-taint,
    I roam, a happy simple-hearted child;
I lightly wander on the hills away,
    Or careless loiter by the meadow streams,
To pluck sweet garlands from the blushing May,—
    The hours all golden with enchanted dreams.

I hear once more the voices of my youth.
 The mystic voices that have long been hushed;
I dream again the dreams of love and truth.
 Again am happy in all hope and trust:
Oh, still as glad as in the vanished Spring
 My heart would tremble to some olden thrill,
If thou wouldst sing me as thou erst didst sing
 Thy mournful vesper by my window-sill.

Why dost thou linger in the far-off land
 When the gay songsters of the wood are here?
What leafy bowers by Spring's warm zephyrs fanned
 Make but a long glad Summer of thy year?
Dost seek green haunts where shadows of the palm
 Shut ever out the noontide's fiercer reign,
Mid spicy groves all prodigal of balm
 That breathe a fragrance on the Indian Main?

Oh, could I journey with thy pinions fleet —
 Swift wing with thee to far-off Southern Isles!
From saddened memories free, what joy to greet
 Each scene of beauty that thy wing beguiles;
There might I find hid in the wild afar
 Some spot untrodden by the feet of Care;
Where Love might linger with no ill to mar,
 No grief to darken, and no wrong to bear.

SEA-SHELLS.

O DWELLERS in the deeps,
Up from the caves of Ocean hither borne!
  Like to the soul that keeps
Forevermore, though in a realm forlorn,
    All memories
Of fore- known love and joy — ye sigh and mourn
And wail for the unfathomable seas.

  I low mine ear incline:
Within your convolutions sway and swash
  All voices of the brine;
I hear on barren reefs the surges dash,
    The breakers roar;
The homeless billows fret and foam and wash,
  And die far off upon an alien shore.

And ye do more complain,
When angry tides with Wintry tempests toss,
   Of ill and wrong and pain;
Like heart new sorrowed at some olden loss,
     Ye moan and sigh
As ye were sore a wounded albatross,
  Or ye would feign the stormy petrel's cry.

    From archipelagoes
That lave the sands of Indra, and the isles
   Of palm, where nightly glows
The sea with a translucent splendor — smiles
     In flash and foam
On shores Australian — over all the miles
  To ye come visions of a long-lost home:

    Telling of all things fair —
Of beauty blooming in the depths below;
   Of coral gardens rare
Where sea-bells, sea-pinks, and sea-roses blow;
     Where twinkle fine
The lamp-auricules; where sea-pens glow,
  And sea-anemones and star-fish shine.

Where to the floor of rock
The limpet clings; where periwinkles hide
From the rude billows' shock;
Where pearly nautilus from prow of pride
Strikes his frail oars,
Or argonaut gay sails the tranquil tide,   ·
Or far below his painted shallop moors.

Down where the diver bold
Takes his lone way, all gems of ocean are:
What marvels yet untold!—
Cones, wattles, volutes, helmets, nerites,—rare
Wonders of God's
Sea-world!—harps, tiaras, ear-shells fair.
With all your kindred of the caverned floods.

There in your home with these
Again to be, ye grieve incessantly;
What deathless sympathies,
Outreaching mortal pain!—what subtle tie.
Unsundered, though
The springs that feed the briny wells go dry.
And mountains flee, and suns wax pale and go!

Though uninterpreted,
What tongue of prophecy, what mystic tone.
    What voice as from the dead;
What intimation of a world unknown —
        A rarer sphere
Transcending all — the still uncharted zone
    That vain we seek, so far and yet so near!

    .   Though all things fade apace,
Do fade and fall, they pass not utterly;
        Within your jasper vase
There lingers still a tone, a mystery. - -
        A something hides
Of glory fled, of love that cannot die:
    All Life that ever was somewhere abides.

        O weary waiting soul!
Thou art not in thy loneliness alone;
        Wherever billows roll.
Or sunlight falls, or pilgrim night-winds moan
        On desert sand,
Some spirit wanders, yearning for its own.
    And unforgotten far-off Fatherland.

7

O exiled from the sea,
That homesick wander from your kin and clime!
What am I more than ye?
Like ye, Life's foregone heritage sublime
I wait and weep:
A polyp, fainting on the shores of Time.
Vain longing for the illimitable deep.

PHEBE.

Last morn, while wrapped in dreamy doze,
   There came — or so it seemed to me —
   The once familiar voice and free
   Of one I may no longer see;
Yet ere I might, as glad I rose,
With greetings fit, my door unclose,
   Came answer from the porch, " Phe-be."

As wakes some long-forgotten word
   Far heard in childhood's Eden clime,
   Or softly pealing Sabbath-chime
   That makes the parted years sublime,
Though but by inmost spirit heard,
So came thy note, thou lowly bird,
   Across the barren moors of Time.

Companion dear of Summers dead,
    Spring's earliest herald, winged and fleet:
    Though not the friend I yearned to greet,
    No less I give thee welcome meet,
Nor mourn the fairer vision fled;
For of these lesser joys is fed
    The hope that waits a joy complete.

Thanks that my weaker care is chid;
    In blithesome scorn of sleet and snow
    I had not thought to meet thee so,
    Before the April violets blow:
But good and ill alike are hid:
Our happiness comes all unbid,
    And takes unchartered wings to go.

What compass guides thy airy quest
    Far over seas that storm and gloam?
    What longings prompt thy wing to roam?
    What yearnings to thy bosom come
To seek the dear remembered nest?
What heart is in that tiny breast,
    So human in its love of home?

Oh sing, oh sing me once again .
    Thy homely " Phe-be " tenderly;
    Nor let thy note, erst warbled free,
    Less joyous wake, that unto me
It bears an undertone of pain —
A vanished Winter's sad refrain
    Blent with the Summer's minstrelsy.

Soon shall thy lays, as oft of old,
    Sweet lullabies in matron tongue
    To dewy morns be softly sung;
    With fragrance-laden roses hung,
Thy old-time nest, now hushed and cold,
Shall new love's priceless treasures hold —
    Be clamorous with thy callow young.

Oh for thy free unsorrowed wing
    To flee these wintry haunts of pain!
    Alas, it were but journeying vain:
    No Summers from the spicy main
May to our fainting spirits bring
The breath of unforgotten Spring —
    Our broken households build again.

KATYDID.

ERE the sumachs crimson turning
Or the upland maples burning
   Show a faintest tint of red;
While the primrose still is glowing,
And the faded pansies sowing
Seed for other seasons' blowing,
   Wakes thy piping, Katydid.

Through the dusky twilight falling
Do I hear thee lonesome calling,
   In thy grassy covert hid;
Of the minstrels of the Summer
. Droning, dolorous, latest comer,
   Autumn's earliest herald-drummer
   Art thou, mournful Katydid.

Sadly falls thy ceaseless sighing
On the heart where hope is dying,
    On the heart where love is dead;
Like an endless wail of sorrow,
Plaint of grief that may not borrow
Solace from the coming morrow —
    Solemn - trilling Katydid.

Ever till our life be ended,
With the higher life inblended,
    From all darkened memories hid,
But to hear thy harp at even,
As in days to sorrow given
Shall our hearts be newly riven;
    Still to mind us, Katydid.

Of the watching. wan and weary,
Through the long hours sad and dreary.
    Tearful eye and sleepless lid;
Watching orbs belovèd, failing
Like the Star of Morning, paling.
Listening dear lips' fevered wailing,
    And thy moaning, Katydid.

Watching by the darkened river,
Slowly ebbing, ebbing ever,
　　Through the midnight dim and dread,
Feet of loved ones, fair as fleeting,
From the shores of Time retreating,
Harkening to our own heart - beating,
　　And thy joyless "Katydid."

Weary, woful, prayerful, tearful,
Waiting sad the moment fearful —
　　Knowing our belovèd dead;
In Death's awful shadow lying,
Reft, despairing, anguished, dying, —
Oh, how cheerless comes thy sighing
　　To the love - lorn, Katydid!

Me — alas! the song ye sing me
Doth such mournful memories bring me
　　Of the days to sorrow wed,
Olden loss doth new bereave me,
Olden griefs new deeply grieve me;
Hush thy requiem - chant, and leave me
　　Unto Silence, Katydid.

SUNRISE BY THE SEA.

To GREET the rising day
    The waiting sea puts all her glory on:
The slow departing shadows, dim and gray,
    More pale and wan,
Far to their gloomy caverns hurrying flee:
As thousand tongues in voiceless melody
    Sing "Hail thou morning sun!"

Porphyry, amethyst,
    Jasper and ruby in one brightness blent,
Gay banners paint for Nature's royalest
    Hierophant;
The weary winds a little space do rest.
While faint and far pulses the billows' breast —
    Throbbing in deep content.

8

Out of the shining wave,
    Slow mounting thence, robed in empurpled gold,
Comes forth the King of Day — lingers to lave
    That brow so old
And yet so young, in the translucent tide;
Lingers like bridegroom by the willing bride,
    When loving arms enfold.

Yet why so late to flee?
    Some message for the loved ones far below?
Some parting kiss for one we may not see?
    Bright rising, lo!
Up from the deep, robed in immortal charms,
A rarer orb, clasped in thy mighty arms,
    As loth to let thee go.

Forgetting love's disguise
    In love's entrance, O lord of Potentates!
Low on the tide that peerless crescent lies:
    Than on thee waits
A fairer queen and consort may not be. —
Fairer than Venus rising from the sea.
    Parting the pearly gates.

"One moment more!" — and still
 "One moment more, oh yet my love delay!"
I hear, or so meseems: — oh for the thrill.
 The rapture — aye
The full impassioned madness of that bliss
That never, far - uprising, shalt thou miss,
 Climbing the hills of Day!

"One moment more!" — ah me!
 How vain to paint love's pure ecstatic glow
Supern, that only the immortals see —
 That mortals know
As the lorn beggar riches; as lost soul
Knows heavenly peace, that hears despairing toll —
 "Down to the depths below!"

" Oh, still one moment more!"
 Yet while I list, loosed are the arms that twine;
The vision fades, as through some open door
 A face divine
Looks on us and is gone; — the sun straightway
Climbs high the regal heavens, and leads the day
 With a serener shine.

And higher still, and higher;
    Still unto heights all meaner heights above,
Let evermore thy kindling feet aspire,
    Thou mighty Jove!
A mightier than he of mythic fame,
Swift bearing wide the torch and oriflamme
    Of an undying love.

Down in the purple deep
    How unto one the long hours lightly wing,
Who there for thee love's tryst doth nightly keep;
    Oh, who may bring
Up thence some hint of her transcendent bliss,
As brooding glad that last embrace and kiss
    Of thee, her lord and king?

Thou that dost make the day,
    If at love's threshold dear thou stoop'st to claim
One parting kiss, though long thy steps delay,
    I may not blame;
Nor will I doubt thy fires eternal burn,
Now that my eyes have seen the hidden urn
    Of all their quenchless flame.

Still onward speed apace!
I may not marvel more, O mighty sun,
Thou never tir'st—wading the deeps of space
    Till day is done;
Remembering so the fairer orb that waits
To greet thee at the bright Hesperian Gates,
    When thy far race is run.

Note.— The preceding poem was suggested by a phenomenon — as rare as
it is remarkable — witnessed by the writer in 1871, upon the shore of Lake
Michigan: when by some mirage or optical illusion, the sun, as it rose from
the lake, appeared attended by a consort or duplicate orb.

THE HAPPY VALLEY.

The World we behold is the Shadow of Life;
    All things are of Being the outward impress;
      Sits a Sphinx by each path that we tread;
    If like a true Sibyl one riddle we guess,
Still ever within, with the Infinite rife,
      Is there hidden a secret unread.

And meaning the inmost — the truest may be
    To the mind and the heart — if outwardly wrought
      Is of Truth but a spectre and wraith;
    The type can but symbol the inflowing thought;
Each soul, as it needs, to its own finds the key —
      And true Love is the key to true Faith.

THE HAPPY VALLEY.

EREWHILE when these hills that slope gentle and fair
Were mountains so high they seemed lightly to bear
 The sky in their rocky embrace;
When all the year long in its beauty unrolled
The meadow its green, wore the harvest its gold,
 The Summer its glory and grace;

Then eyes they were clear, for the world it was new,
And ever the marvellous stories were true
 That cannot be wholly forgot;
Then silver and gold, though they never were found,
In treasures uncounted were hid in the ground,
 And dragons watched over the spot.

In river and wood dwelt sylphs, naiads, and fays,
Were everywhere seen in those wonderful days —
 Though fled is the Faëry race;
And who in this world is so spotless and good
To blame the sweet tenants of river and wood
 For hiding each beautiful face?

At eve, all the far-lapsing billows along
The mermaiden sang, and so charmèd a song
    That hushed was each murmuring wave;
And who harkened that dangerous minstrelsy
Went with her, alas! to her home in the sea—
    To her home in a coral cave.

Then every maid was a shepherdess bold,
Yet gentle as was gentlest lamb in her fold;
    So learned in Love's magical art
She could marry a prince whenever she would.
With a boundless estate, and noble and good.
    And reign a proud queen of the heart.

In those marvellous days that all wonder enfold.
Bright days that illumine each legend of old
    As sundown the westering main.
Far on the blue seas loomed with wave-warded strand
A mountain-girt, summer-clad, love-guarded land.
    Undarkened of discord and pain.

Though where may be hidden the Beautiful Vale
Where care is unknown, where no sorrows assail,—
    If isled on wide oceans afar,
I know not;—perchance it lies under the sea
Twice ten thousand fathoms;—though still it may be
    Where gates of the Morning unbar.

Howbeit — though shut from the wide world apart,
There prodigal Nature with kindliest art
    Her gifts in such affluence poured.
That looking anear on each scene of delight
You had thought it an Eden unsorrowed of blight
    Or to its lost beauty restored.

The hillside was gay with the citron and clove,
The olive tree grew with the fig in the grove,
    The orange o'erburdened with scent;
The evening-born zephyr winged faint with perfume,
The orchard boughs reddened, adight with new bloom,
    As low with ripe fruitage they bent.

By emerald sands, amid islands of calm,
Its shimmering track overshadowed with palm,
    A river meandering went;
Went limpid and clear through the meadows along,
Went dallying, singing a lullaby song —
    A murmur and song of content.

Free wandered the flocks, with their fleeces of snow
As white as the storm-girded Winter might show
    Aloft in his silvery tent,
To new-springing pastures so luscious and green,
Or gaily anon might be frolicking seen
    As on to the mountains they went.

Thence sweetly their bleating like music would fall,
As homeward they came at each shepherdess' call,
    When twilight its shadows had cast;
Where yielding their milk-bearing udders, they lent
The joy-waiting cottager's home of content
    The evening's delicious repast.

Where hearts all untainted of passion and strife
Grew guilelessly up in love's summering life.
    That brightened from portal to roof
Each sylvan-wrought home, unadornèd and plain.
From pleasures that leave in the bosom a stain
    And vainer illusions aloof.

Whence forth at the morn, ever joyous and gay,
Went maidens and youths to the harvest away
    Where golden it gleamed in the sun;
Or charmed the glad twilight with love-breathing lute.
Or lingered to dance to the tymbal and flute,
    When the day with its labors was done.

May love so illumine the homeliest cot,
So charmed with content be the lowliest lot.
    That sorrow may never assail?
And was the true secret of happiness known —
Lost secret, alas! — to that people alone
    Who dwelt in the Beautiful Vale?

I know not: Lost Land, on far tropical sea
Haply shining serene, if only in thee,
    Still lit with affections unchanged,
Are thresholds so bright that no shadows may cross,
Are hearthstones undarkened with anguish and loss —
    Where lovers are never estranged.

And well you had doubted, one home to have seen,
Where joy ever wore its perennial green,
    If Heaven has happier ones;
So rich without pride, without envy or blame,
So rich in the truest wealth woman may claim —
    The treasure of beautiful sons.

Nor alone in the sunlight of motherly eyes:
For maidens, though hooded in maiden disguise,
    Looked on them with partialest joy;
On Jehan the husbandman valiant and bold,
On Clarence the dreamer, that tended the fold,
    And Reuben the studious boy.

So tranquil the skies were that over them bent,
They nigh unto manhood had journeyed content,
    Nor tasted of pleasures unmeet;
Still slumbered desire in each peace-tented breast —
Desire that might waken the wish and unrest
    To stray from that charmèd retreat.

That world all unknown — was it sombre and dread,
That wide from that rock - builded barrier spread,
    Or sunny and mossy and green,
With mountains and valleys, and peopled with men?
None ever had passed, thence returning again,
    To tell of each wonderful scene.

A perilous way to him journeying there;
For lo! by the path that his footsteps must dare,
    A cleft where a mountain had stood,
A fiery Dragon, by night and by day,
A fiery Dragon stood guarding the way —
    Stood belching a fiery flood.

And he that would venture that Valley beyond
Must a talisman bear — a magical wand
    The truly wise only may gain;
While he that would pass, said a prophet of old,
Unlearned in the secret, though fearless and bold,
    Would sure by that Dragon be slain.

And why should there come to the dream-haunted heart
The wish from that beautiful home to depart,
    Untroubled of sorrow or care?
And where in the wide world without and unknown
Were youths that to manlier stature had grown,
    Or maidens more gentle and fair?

Yet had we the wings that could cleave the broad blue,
The pinions of Morning, and though it were true
    We dwelt in an Eden of bliss,
How swift would we climb the bright ether afar,
If only to see if yon tiniest star
    A world is, and fairer than this.

For deep in the soul the aspiring abides
To question each secret in Nature that hides —
    Forever for knowledge athirst.
Not Heaven alone would it fearless explore,
But dauntless would tread the Plutonian Shore
    And map the dark regions accursed.

Nor wonder the youth, on some star-guided trail
Far wandering alone in that Beautiful Vale,
    Might dream of that magical wand:
And question if Cynthia, just hidden from sight
By high-beetling mountains, the peerless, might light
    A fairer world lying beyond.

Nor alone in the light that so silvery shone,
That far world grew fairer — that far world unknown.
    To Jehan, the longer he dreamed;
Till beauty anear had no beauty for him;
Noon's radiant sunshine with shadows was dim;
    The horizon narrower seemed.

No longer he led in the dance of delight.
No longer his lute charmed the listening night,
    Nor songs cheered the lingering day;
Still brooded that shadow when toiling afield;
More darkly it deepened when midnight revealed
    That Dragon dread guarding the way.

Still dreaming, and leaving his labor undone,
Chance guided, or led by the westering sun,
    . Or lured by that fatuous ray —
That vision of beauty — O fatal unrest! —
With quickening footsteps he eagerly pressed
    The path to the mountain away.

The loftiest peak that far dazzled and shone,
High lifted alluring its snow - mantled cone
    O'er valley and river and wood;
Still toiling aloft on each intricate trail,
While dim and more dim shone the Beautiful Vale,
    Upon the tall summit he stood.

When lo! from that airy empyrean height,
What realm of enchantment arose on his sight!
    Elysian fields glimmer and gleam,
Enshrouding in gloom evermore to his eye
That Valley. close shut by the mountains so high; —
    And this was the land of his dream!

There seeming to reach unto limitless day,
A new world, that broadened unbounded away.
     Unto his rapt vision unrolled;
Where palaces shone, of all pleasures the shrine,
And gardens and fountains and statues divine
     Gay glittered with crystal and gold.

Enrapt with the splendor and glory he saw,
He lingered, still gazing in wonder and awe
     Till night-mists enshrouded the scene;
Then downward again through the darkness and gloam
Returning, he passed to his once happy home —
     Alas, now how homely and mean!

The mother who saw, with a motherly care,
Beneath the disguises that sorrow would wear,
     Her joy-loving Jehan was sad,
Besought him, if ill had befallen to know —
If ill or misfortune had burdened with woe
     The heart ever wont to be glad.

Said Jehan, "Our home is a prison; its ward
That Fiery Dragon, accursed and abhorred;
     On cottage and meadow and lea
Forever the gloom and the shadows do lie,
Foreboding and dark, of the mountains so high;
     And long have I yearned to be free.

"I climbed to their cloud-mantled summit to-day:
More fair than I dreamed is that far world away;
    There lie, with gold-glittering strand,
The Isles of Delight, with all splendors aglow;
The home of all pleasures; — to-morrow I go
    To dwell in that beautiful land.

"A holiday life, a perpetual joy,
No toiling to trouble, no want to annoy;
    Such plenty this poverty mocks;
Such pleasures and riches we never may guess
Who only the fruits of our orchards possess —
    The fleeces and milk of our flocks."

O fatalest vision of beauty! his sight.
If only it were in a dream of the night,
    Beyond the horizon had flown;
Already his footsteps were wandering free:
Ere long, and a palace of crystal should be
    His home in that new world unknown.

The mother but sighed, "All illusive and vain;"
Yet felt in her heart the foreboding of pain
    That ever some sorrow betides;
Nor hastily chiding his purpose unwise,
Bent tenderly on him love's pitying eyes.
    Whose lid the tear tremblingly hides;

To soon overflow with its anguish and pain
For treasure the years may not render again —
    For loss Time may never requite;
For oh! at the dawn, he, her Jehan, would tread
The perilous way past that barrier dread,
    To dwell in the Land of Delight.

So luring the vision that beckoned away.
Unheeded the tears that besought him to stay —
    The mother's low - murmuring sigh:
"Oh, why should I live but this day to behold?
Ah me! that the Siren of Pleasure or Gold
    Should sever Love's beautiful tie!

" Yet harken and know, if my counsels are vain:
None ever may pass till that Dragon be slain;
    Say, have you that talisman won?
None ever may venture the Valley beyond
But he whose hand beareth that magical wand —
    Remember. my son. O my son!"

No answer he gave; but the earliest dawn
Looked down on that cottage, and Jehan was gone:
    At sunrise, more fierce than before,
That Dragon. mad - glaring and bloody the same.
Wide vomited torrents of sulphurous flame, —
    And Jehan was heard of no more.
       *   *   *

When Time with soft healing a solace had lent,
The Mother glad smiled in her home of content.
    As one that no sorrow had crossed:
Yet oft when the day on the mountain was dim.
Her eye thence turned tearful: her thought was of him
    Her first-born — of Jehan. the lost.

Albeit the heart, every burden resigned,
For pain and bereavement the sorest. shall find
    A balm in the medicined years;
Yet oh, if for grief but this comfort accrue.
The swift-winging moments still open anew
    Forever the fountain of tears.

And woe to the widowed! — one grief overpassed
Is only of sorrows one nearer the last:
    New stricken with anguish untold,
Her Clarence she saw by the hearth's paling light
Sit brooding that vision. illusive as bright.
    That lost her her Jehan of old.

A joy in his labor no longer he found,
But more, as the days wore monotonous round.
    He pensive and silent became;
Like Jehan, he climbed to that cloud-mantled height
Like Jehan, he gazed on that Land of Delight,
    With yearnings and longings the same.

He saw the world broaden so boundless away,
Where moved the vast throng in their brilliant array,
    The horizon looming immense.
With billowy seas to his wondering view,
With lands still beyond in the limitless blue,
    Far shining more luminous thence.

The sunset had left all the mountain aflame,
As down to the night-glooming Valley he came:
    How mean seemed the life he had led!
How rude and unsightly that cottage, his home —
His home now no longer, for he too would roam,
    That land of enchantment would tread.

The Mother, whose heart bore the prescient pain
Of sorrow-foreboding, besought him in vain:
    " What good can my darling desire?
Oh, what has befallen my Clarence to-day —
So wont to be cheerful and tuneful and gay?
    Why slumber his songs and his lyre?"

"Our Valley is small," said the youth in reply;
"The horizon narrow, the mountains so high
    The shadows lie darkly below;
That far world away — oh how peerless and grand!
My feet will not rest from that beautiful land; —
    To-morrow, to-morrow I go!"

Love answered him weeping: "What more do you know
Than he that was lost in the days long ago—
    My first-born, my beautiful son?
Oh, why will you venture the mountain to pass,
Again to o'erwhelm me with sorrow—alas!
    Say, have you that talisman won?"

"Yea, Mother, for mine is a worthier quest,"
Said Clarence; "this burning desire in my breast
    No thought of mere pleasure has fanned;
I go for no purpose ignoble and vain;
I bear, in the wish and the longing to gain
    All knowledge, that magical wand."

Low bent, as thrice widowed, the Mother again
Sat weeping till Midnight looked in at the pane.
    Sad harkened her sorrowing wail;
For knew she how false, how deceitful the charm
Of knowledge—that knowledge might never disarm
    That guardian fierce of the Vale.

The eyes of the Morning, all tearful and red,
Bent mournful on Reuben, as lonely he led
    His flocks to their pastures so green;
More fierce and mad-glaring and bloody the same,
That Dragon stood belching wide torrents of flame:
    And Clarence—he never was seen.

And in the glad Summers that beautiful wore,
His name in that Valley was spoken no more:
    Or only, her loss to bemoan,
To Reuben, the Mother's now only delight,
Was whispered, and softly, as sadly at night
    They mused by the fireside alone.

O heart of the Mother! forever to bear
Its infinite sorrow of love and despair!
    Howbeit, but darkly we know:
Yet ever some truth in Tradition is found,
And many, alas! by that Dragon lie bound —
    Bound fast in a region of woe.

And oft when the Midnight shone angry and red,
Came sounds from afar, as of anguish and dread,
    Lamenting and sorrowing vain:
While ever anon, fearful borne on the air,
Came tumult of battle, the wail of despair,
    The moaning of spirits in pain.

    *   *   *

The earth mantles green that the earthquake has rent;
The hills shine new-verdured when Winter is spent;
    New bourgeons with sweetness the grove; —
So kindles anew in the desolate years
The day-star of Hope, quenched in anguish and tears,
    Re-lit with the sunshine of Love.

The Mother erelong, not to sorrow in vain.
Took up all her love-bearing burdens again —
    Though widowed, not wholly bereft;
Though, telling of griefs for the loves she had lost,
Her brow wore a circlet of silver and frost,
    More joyed she in one that was left.

And patient at evening, at morning, and noon,
Her spindle she plied, with its musical tune
    Beguiling the care in her breast;
Yet oft, when the twilight fell sober and pale,
Would tears, with sad memories burdened, unveil
    Unbidden, the sorrowful guest.

And is there an ever unmedicined woe?
Howbeit we know not; this only we know:
    When breaks on the desolate years
Some loss that Time never may lighten again,
How dull seems the smart of a sorrow whose pain
    May yield to the solace of tears!

And what unto her, the thrice-widowed, was left?
Alas! to that bosom so sorely bereft
    The sorrow of sorrows had come;
The last of her treasures — her staff and her joy —
Her Reuben, her comfort, her studious boy,
    Sat joyless and dreaming and dumb.

O eyes of the Mother! what pleading and prayer!
O heart of the Mother, unbroken to bear
    Of love the remembered caress!
What bodings of ill all the future bethrong.
Well knowing, dream-haunted, his footsteps ere long
    That path of enchantment would press.

What marvel to him would the morrow unveil?
At dawn he had passed on the mountain-led trail
    With light-speeding footsteps and bold;
On him the bright world of immensity smiled,
Whose glories illusive so fatal beguiled —
    Lost Jehan and Clarence of old.

Fair broadened the same to his wondering sight
The boundless horizon; the Land of Delight
    In limitless splendor unrolled;
Where threshold and portal and pillar and dome
Of many a palace, of pleasure the home,
    Gay glittered with crystal and gold.

Rapt in wonder and awe a moment he stood,
Nor questioned the pageant if evil or good,
    Allured with its shimmer and sheen;
But gazing intent, with his sight clearer grown,
In a world that to others so beautiful shone
    He saw but a sorrowful scene.

He saw in that new world so seemingly fair
No brow but was dark with the shadow of care,
    Though dwelling mid splendors untold;
Each phantom delight that evanishing rose
Was but the delirious frenzy of those
    Whose gods are but pleasure and gold.

Palace, pillar, and dome, with their glitter and glow,
All things he beheld, were but treacherous show;
    The gardens of beauty and bloom
Bore only the fruit that is bitter to taste;
The blossoms — if blossoms there brightened the waste,
    Were poppies of deadly perfume.

An innermost life with true being is wed:
As this, so the outward is, living or dead, —
    The living alone shall remain;
Whatever of Truth or of Beauty there hides
In the soul, in the world is in which it abides;
    All else is illusive and vain.

His footsteps delayed on the rock - builded height,
Till loftier purpose that sorrowing sight
    Awoke in his pitying breast:
And he too would go — every danger would dare,
Might he the true secret of happiness bear
    Afar to that people unblest.

Grew stronger and deeper that worthier aim,
As downward he passed — to the cottage he came.
    To dream of that magical wand;
If only by him might the Dragon be slain!
Still deeply he pondered that vision of pain —
    That charmed but illusory land.

The Mother, low bowed in new terror and dread,
Bent on him, as silent we look on the dead;
    For well, without question, she guessed
That he too, her Reuben, that border would pass —
His footsteps the path to the mountain, alas!
    That path of enchantment had pressed.

Nor more did she weep, for the fountain of tears
Within her was dry with the sorrow of years;
    Nor minded the pitying Dawn,
Though all the long night of her anguish was spent
Low moaning, as o'er the dead embers she bent,
    "Oh he, my last treasure, is gone!"

Rain torrents of flame on his venturous head!
Make fiery the pathway he fearless must tread,
    Who passes that Valley beyond!
Weave, evil-taught demons, your sorcerous thrall!
Yet him, midst all perils, no ill shall befall,
    If bearing that magical wand.

When tardy the Morning, and mournful, at last
Looked down on the Valley, thence Reuben had passed.
    Had passed at the earliest sheen;
But lo! when the Day on the mountain was bright —
Had drowned all the sombering shadows with light.
    That Dragon no longer was seen.

Dim rising afar on her tear-darkened view,
What wonder is there? — could her vision be true?
    The Mother rejoices again:
That Dragon, that ever by night and by day
Stood barring the path to that far world away,
    That Dragon her Reuben had slain!

And still as she gazed, lo! what marvels unfold?
What splendors break fair over woodland and wold?
    More bright, with a lovelier bloom,
Earth, thrilling ecstatic, quick mantles and glows;
Arrayed in new beauty, each flower that blows
    Is sweet with a rarer perfume.

More golden the harvest that billows the plain,
With sound of the sickle blends happier strain
    That joyous the reapers prolong:
The groves stand enrapt, with new blossoms adight,
More tremulous thrill with a sense of delight —
    Are vocal with happier song.

All Nature, endowed with a tenderer grace,
Like angel of mercy, that seeks to erase
    All record of error and blame.
Glad kindles and quickens with beauty, until
Field, meadow, and woodland, and valley, and hill,
    The triumph of Virtue proclaim.

      *   *   *

Not he that would be of all Riches possessed,
Nor he that would pass of all Knowledge in quest,
    Might venture that Valley beyond;
He only that spell of enchantment withstood
Who sought not his own, but of others the good:
    Lore — Lore was that Magical Wand.

SONGS OF THE SEASONS.

Though all things with the changeful Seasons flee,
  A garland glorious in its odorous shine
  A few fleet sunny Summer hours may twine,
    To fade, then spring again
      In sun and shine —
    The myriad lowly blooms on hill and plain;
While evermore the changeful Seasons flee —
      Forever onward flee.

The thoughts that light the temple of the Soul,
  The fire that burns upon its inner shrine,
  The love and faith that from its depths outshine, —
    That shall not all depart,
      But bloom and twine
    In Winters as in Summers of the heart;
These mark the years unto the living Soul —
      The ever-living Soul.

O ROSE, whose tiny buds enfold
    The promise of a perfect flower;
    O Tulip, that a precious dower
Of beauty in thy heart dost hold;
O Lily, that a robe of gold
    Art weaving for thy bridal hour;

Ye Hyacinths, whose petals show
    More than the blue of Summer skies;
    Ye Pansies that so fair arise
And smile on April's sleet and snow;
Ye Violets that bashful show
    The heaven that is in loving eyes;

And all ye waiting blooms that sleep
    The sleep by rarest dreams beguiled;
    Ye children of, the wood and wild
That watch, but do not watch and weep;—
Oh for the simple trust ye keep!
    Your saintly faith, O undefiled!

Though fierce the stormy tempest rage,
    Ye only hear the murmuring
    Of Summer, like the dreams that bring
The vision of Love's golden age;.
And thrill to rapture's dim presage,
    The pulse and prophecy of Spring.

Oh for your patient "All is well;"
    Though shrouded deep in gloom and night,
    Of radiant hours of dear delight
Your dimly-folded petals tell,
As wing, dark brooding in the shell,
    Foreshows a free aërial flight.

O heart of mine! and art thou less
    Than flower the kindly soil inurns?
    The faithful sun to it returns—
Thy proper good thou shalt not miss;
More than a paradise of bliss
    Lives in the soul that loves and yearns.

SEED-TIME.

OH, THIS the Toiler's happy fate:
  He shall not toil in vain;
So, toiling early, toiling late,
  Till well the gleby plain;
Cast in the fruitful seed and wait
  The sunshine. dew, and rain;
Though many a morn shall come and go,
  And night succeed the day,
Full-eared the ripened sheaf shall glow
  In Autumn's halcyon ray.

Nor less, with labor made sublime
  By purpose true and strong,
Sow all the fallow fields of Time
  With Thought and Deed and Song;
And trust, from farthest land and clime,
  The waiting heart erelong
Shall gather in its harvest hoard
  Of precious corn and oil,
And wine of love, to brim the board—
  Make glad the after-toil.

A SONG OF MAY.

THERE'S a harp in the boughs of the lindens again,
    Like the voices my infancy knew;
There are tiny throats trilling a joyous refrain
    To the morning bejewelled with dew;
And the dear baby-buds that all beauty enfold,
    Softly peep from their covert to-day;
Lo! the Hyacinth's purple and Daffodil's gold
    Are unveiling the glory of May.

There are Cowslips bestarring the moor-meadow green,
    Budding Buttercups pale with surprise;
Sunny Dandelions couched in their velvety screen
    Are outlooking with wondering eyes;
While the sweet-bringing bee in the orchard a-hum
    Vagrant loiters the noon-tide away,
Till the drone of his piping with sweetness is dumb
    In the bountiful blossoms of May.

There are Violets dear that have been with us long —
  Spring's first darlings from under the snow;
And the frailer Anemones haply prolong
  Vanished April's ephemeral show;
Far the Dogwood is showering its snow in the dells,
  And the Hazel with tassels is gay;
Softly rings the Azalia its silvery bells
  To the rivulet's murmur of May.

And the Tulip I see, in the pride of her bloom, —
  She has put on her gaudiest suit
For the Lilac, outbreathing a luscious perfume
  To the Strawberry's promise of fruit;
High the Iris is bearing his helmet and spear —
  Fair unfolding his azuring ray;
While the sigh of the slumbering Roses I hear,
  All impatient of lingering May.

Yet how vain is the charm of each murmurous lute,
  Vain the dower of all beauty, to him
Who must mourn the sweet music of lips that are mute
  And the sunshine of eyes that are dim;
In each flowering bell, through each chorister's throat,
  Sings the Summer a sorrowing lay
To the heart that still misses Love's rapturing note
  From the merriest anthems of May.

JUNE.

Month of Flora! month of roses!
 Bring again the gifts divine:
Autumn's gold thy heart encloses;—
 In the garlands thou dost twine
Hides the heaping Horn of Plenty—brims the vintage-
    glowing wine.

When the dewy dawn is breaking
 Unto morn serene and grand.
Hark! exultant anthem waking
 Of the wildwood's warbling band,
Like a wind-swept harp Æolian, joyful thrilling all the
    land.

High the Thrush his song is swelling
 Where no meaner voice intrudes:
Far the Wood-dove's note is telling
 Love's soft matin through the woods.
While a home of beauty building mid the leafy solitudes.

Mad with Joy's delirium panting,
   Nearer sings the Oriole;
Loud the Bobolink is chanting
   "Bob-o-link," with fiery soul,
Till through all the woodland arches wide the music
   billows roll.

Lowly minstrels! long above ye
   Gently wave the budding sprays;
Never will I cease to love ye;—
   Let your choral roundelays
Waken still Love's wild aspirings, yearnings for harmo-
   nious days.

Though the Seasons swiftly leave us,
   Each some precious boon shall bring;
Nor shall ever Hope deceive us
   Waiting for the coming Spring—
Waiting for the promised Summer, with its light and
   blossoming.

AUTUMN FLOWERS.

Though but a memory is the flowery reign
    Of gentle Spring, out of the days before;
And Summer, journeying over hill and plain,
      By sea and shore,
Jewelled and crowned, leading a joyous train.
    And gorgeous, is no more:—

Still unto Autumn suns is beauty born:
    One Artist-hand paints every flower that blows:
The garlands that October's brow adorn
      Are dear as those
By lovely June in all her glory worn.
    Crowned with the royal Rose.

The garden boasts the Dahlia's regal show;
    The many-hued Verbenas glint and shine:
Uplifts the Feverfew its brow of snow:
      Still climb and twine
The Morning-glories; Portulacas glow—
    Flame like a ruby-mine.

And all the common flowers — a lowly race —
 Their bloom prolong: — the Zinnias bright unfold:
The Cockscomb proud flaunts high each gaudy grace;
    The Marigold,
Though rude and homely, wears the cheerful face
 It wore in days of old.

The Primrose frail, like her the Summer knew,
  Hides from the ardor and the glare of noon;
Bears to the stars, as erst she poured unto
    The Harvest-moon,
The fervor of a passionate heart and true
 Though paling all too soon.

In borders wide the Asters radiant bloom —
 For beauty's lofty guerdon vie and cope;
The wind that murmurs by the Violet's tomb
    Of vanished hope.
Comes laden with the Mignonette's perfume
 And breath of Heliotrope.

Still keeps the Amaranth. nor overworn,
 The loveliness that saw the Summer come:
And one shall glad the Christmas hour adorn —
    Chrysanthemum.
Made dearer for the kisses latest-born
 Of lips now cold and dumb.

13

In shady nooks the gentle Pansies show
    A smile as tender as the buds that blew —
Buds born too soon — amid the April snow;
        I wander through
The tranquil woods with Golden Rod aglow,
    And Speedwell's sapphire - hue.

Nor these alone illume the waning hour:
    Along the moor with fierce intensity
Kindles and burns the scarlet Cardinal Flower:
        And hosts there be —
The miscalled weeds, that, dowered with beauty's dower.
    Gleam like a golden sea.

And oh, if chance the tempest's ruder kiss
    Leave all the flowers of Spring untimely sere,
Or drouth lay waste the Summer's loveliness,
        Thrice doubly dear
Are ye, Autumnal blooms! that charm and bless
    The slowly - passing year.

And best beloved, long - sought, late - found, — O mine
    More than this blossomed sweetness, Friend of Fate!
Though on life's hills the hues of Autumn shine.
        All seasons wait
Alike the Rose of Love — the flower divine,
    That never blooms too late.

PARTING SUMMER.

THERE is a moaning on the breath of morn,
A solemn cadence in the rillet's chime,
A voice foreboding on the night-winds borne—
The first low breathing of the wintry time.
The while meek Summer over all things broods
And pensive ponders on each lessening day,
There comes a glory on the ripened woods—
The sure precursor of a swift decay.

The corn is bending to the zephyrs free,
Its thick ears waving with a flush of gold;
The fruit is ripening on each orchard tree,
The nut is browning on the hazel-wold;
But she, the Beauteous, who had hardly known
One tearful trouble, in her sorrow lies;
Her song is saddened in its every tone,
And dimmed the shining of her lustrous eyes.

And when her sceptre from her swaying falls.
   Oh, who would chide her for the brimming tear.
While to our hearts for sympathy she calls.
   Through all the voices of the failing year?
As thrills our being with a sudden pain.
   When fall the shadows of life's closing day.
To find its promise of fruition vain,
   So freely trusted all the coming way:

As stirs the spirit with a dread unrest
   And trails its pinion in the very dust,
As bowed with anguish is the aching breast
   Ere Hope is anchored in a higher trust,—
So is she stricken with the sorest grief:
   And oh, what wonder she should make such moan,
To leave the treasures of a life so brief.
   And all things lovely that are still her own?

Erewhile I marked her as she musing strayed
   Through paths oft trodden in the vanished time
When gaily wandering as the vernal maid.
   Or glad and joyous in her matron prime:
Soft charms still kindled in those features fair.
   Quick feeling trembled in her troubled eye;
Her cheek still mantled through its lines of care.
   Her lip low murmured through each stifled sigh:

"How have I nurtured ye with light and dew.
  Ye woods, far waving with your glossy spray;
Each leaf now fading where it fluttering grew
  Shall soon be wafted by the winds away.
And heaped and moulding in the lonely vale
  With every semblance of its greenness gone,
Or trod by truant on the upland trail.
  Or rustle fearful to the startled fawn.

"And you. ye songsters of the airy wing.
  I well with plenty have your wants supplied;
And still contented could I hear ye sing,
  Nor dream of aught of recompense beside:
But now the voices of the grove are mute,
  Save few more venturous that may still prolong
Joy's dying anthems with a lonely flute —
  And these are singing too their parting song.

"And yon bright lakelets shall I see no more,
  With white waves flashing in the Summer's pride?
Will ye not sadden to the saddened shore,
  With storm-clouds mirrored in your glassy tide?
And you, ye rillets of the silver chime,
  That gleam and sparkle like a love-lit eye.
Will ye not miss me in the coming time,
  And dim and darken to the darkened sky?

" And must I leave you in your beauty all,
    Ye haunts so cherished, of field, wood, and glade,
And know ye shrouded in a gloom and pall,
    A dearth all darkly on your brightness laid?
The earth was starry with my tiny flowers,
    Now lost, or sweetly unto fruitage grown;
That soon, when ripened in the golden hours,
    Shall Autumn garner as if all his own.

"Still would I tarry if I might with these,
    If but in pleasures of the Past to dwell;
I may not rest me but beyond the seas, —
    My reign is ended, and I go: Farewell."
But still she lingered, as if loth to part
    From scene and vision with her being twined;
And how can woman, with a woman's heart,
    Forget each idol that it once hath shrined?

And still she lingered; and I could but mourn
    To see her grieving, and so soon to go; —
But hark! she listens to the sounding horn
    Of Autumn, winding in the vale below:
Startled, she gazes on a stranger crest —
    (She hardly knew him for her tear-dimmed sight);
Then swift reclining on his manly breast,
    Re-gave his greeting with a heart-delight.

And many a day—a long bright sunny time—
  These twain have tarried, and ye could not know
If this were Summer's in her sober prime,
  Or that were Autumn's in his genial glow;
But late I marked him with a ruffled brow,
  A look of sternness in his troubled eyes;
A frown is shrouding their effulgence now,
  And clouds are flying through the startled skies.

Like sparks outpouring from some furnace fire,
  The woods are showering off their crimson locks;
The winds blow boisterous in their fitful ire —
  The first up-gathering of the Equinox.
And she, the Beauteous, with a brow serene,
  As if the calm of heavenly hope it wore,
Gave one look fondly at each olden scene,
  One smile of parting, and was seen no more.

ASPHODEL.

SAD September winds are swelling
   Through the dreary Autumn wood;
As some haunting shade were telling
   Through that regal solitude
Of the Past's untimely perished,
   The beloved of gayer hours,
Early lost, too deeply cherished, —
   Blighted hopes and faded flowers.

Once — what time the bee was drunken
   On the orchard-bough's perfume,
In the Cowslip's calyx sunken,
   Or the Lilac's purple bloom, —
By my path a flower was blowing,
   With the Snow-drops, fair and frail;
A more living beauty growing
   Than the pride of Sharon's Vale.

Ever from its morning natal
    Did my heart all lovingly
Watch each tiny folded petal
    Slow unveil its mystery;
Though, the hours with brightness winging,
    Wheresoe'er the sunlight fell
Were a thousand blooms upspringing,
    None so fair as Asphodel.

*   *   *

But the Mignonette is faded,
    Dimmed the Tulip's gaudy dyes,
And the light of pity shaded
    In the Violet's brimming eyes:
No ambrosia sweetly lingers
    In the Rose's nectar-wells,
And no sound of fairy fingers
    In the faded Lily-bells.

Lone the wood-haunts sleep ungladdened
    With the Speedwell's sapphire blue,
Prone the Clematis lies saddened
    With a love-forsaken hue;
Darkly quenched the frail aspiring
    Of the Jasmine's slender stem;
Thick the clustered Vine is firing
    With the Autumn's diadem;

14

Summer's troubled cheek is paling;
   And my heart, bereft and sore,
With the widowed hours is wailing
   For the Beautiful — no more;
All the garden walks are lonely,
   Waking to no little tread;
All things wore a beauty only
   In the love that now is dead.

Grief, alas! my grief to heighten,
   In my loss is other known;
All earth's fairest gifts do brighten
   With a radiance not their own;
All things beauteous and tender —
   Summer blooms and sunset skies —
Wear alone their Eden splendor
   In the light of loving eyes.

OCTOBER.

Oh how I love ye, pensive Autumn days,
    With suns so meek, so beautiful and brief;
    When grove and tree shed down the crimson leaf.
And Summer birds have sung their parting lays;
When lowly lies each haunt by vale and hill
    In mellow brightness of the hazy skies;
When, as in thought, all Nature hushed and still
    In sober, dreamy melancholy lies.
Why do ye win me so — oh, who may tell?
    As yields the doting heart the deepest trust,
As bows the stubborn will to Beauty's spell,
So do I pour an homage full and free,
    Because I would, but more because I must,
Unto the days the loveliest that be.

AUTUMN.

With radiant brow, though deeply furrowed o'er
With lines of toil, old Autumn, hale appearing,
  As if content with plenty, seeks no more;
  Leans on his staff and eyes his treasured store.
The woe-worn wizard Want no longer fearing;
Broods o'er the Past—each tender thought endearing
  His young loves, now no more.

And who the story of his days may tell,
Each deed and purpose of his heart divining?
  These, like his sheaves, are ripe and garnered well—
  All safely locked in Memory's deepest cell:
Now, like a bough, no golden fruit inclining,
Or leafless tree where no brown nut is shining,
  When all are hoarded well.

And much of gladness, though in life's decline,
Yet warms his breast, in every feature glowing;
    He quaffs a bumper of the choicest wine,
    Still fresh from vintage where the clusters shine;
His full hand freely unto Want bestowing —
O'erjoyed to see the cup of all, high flowing
    With oil and corn and wine.

Yet have I marked him when in pensive mood
Hard by my way on mossy bank reclining;
    But on his rest I never dared intrude, —
    His tearful eye forbade obtrusion rude;
Such snowy locks his kingly forehead twining,
With such a presence all around him shining,
    I never dared intrude.

Though oft when passing with a lingering tread
I could but think the old man's heart was breaking;
    His lips were calling on the loved and dead,
    And free the flowing of the tears he shed;
Now to his sight the Past new beauty taking,
While every thought, unconscious sigh awaking,
    Was of the loved and dead.

And thus he mused: " How long since low we laid
Your faded forms, O loved ones buried lying!
  How many well-endeared doth cypress shade!
  And beauteous Flora — her, the gentlest maid " —
(My own eyes moistened at his tears and sighing)
" Her of the early wed and early dying —
    Her too doth cypress shade.

" My toil-got gold — oh what a bootless gain!
And this the end of all my striving, praying:
  My loves, my hopes, my aspirations vain,
  Outliving all of life itself but pain —
The sense the deepest and the latest staying;
No pitying hand its keenest pang allaying —
    Hopes, aspirations, vain."

While yet his tear-wet eye and heaving breast
Betokened still his grief found no beguiling,
  A lovely form, with grace celestial blest,
  Came softly nigh, and sought his place of rest;
I knew sweet Summer by her kindly smiling,
That oft erewhile, a darkened moment whiling,
    My own lone heart had blest.

She had come back — yes, had come back again,
To olden scenes, serene and calm outlying;
  To linger yet awhile on hill and plain
  Where erst she wandered with a joyous train.
Ere earth's soft music knew a tone of sighing,
Ere bright things saddened at the thought of dying,
  O'er hill or vale or plain.

But not to mourn her youthful visions o'er —
One glorious faith from out their wreck retrieving:
  Though grief at frost and blight were deep and sore,
  That all of Love will live forevermore,
That fadeless wreath eternity is weaving;
But oh! to find her friend so deeply grieving,
  It pained her sad and sore.

That meeting who may paint? — my pen is weak:
The deep, deep pulsing of the heart's revealing
  Is language truer than the tongue can speak,
  Though on expression every power it wreak;
The long, long, warm embrace its fount unsealing —
The ebb and flowing of the tide of feeling
  Leave naught for lips to speak.

. And may not love have home—yea, love refined
In chastened breast with holiest passion swelling?
  Such are the magnet sympathies that bind
  In deeper, closer unity of mind,
The kin of thought—of life whose spirit dwelling
Is in the One Great Heart, whose love outwelling
      For aye doth all things bind.

  Nor strange that gladness should resume her reign,
As with all Hope-charmed words her lips were showing
  The stern though dread necessity of pain—
  How early loss may be our later gain;
While every soothing sympathy bestowing,
Such as alone from woman's heart outflowing
      May loose the bond of pain.

  And I have seen, through many a shining day,
O'er hill and plain these twain together straying,
  While in their eyes gleams such a heavenly ray
  I can but deem their bliss is full alway;
But still I fear me for their transient staying;
Yet would I long, the last farewell delaying,
      Joy in that rapturing ray.

INDIAN SUMMER.

LIKE bannered host, with helmet, plume and spear
Far borne elate, from thousand battles gory,
   The flaming woodlands glow; — these, year by year,
   Are Nature's palimpsest, whereon, austere
In Winter gloom, or gay in Summer glory,
Is writ with magic pen the wondrous story
   Of all the circling year.

How thrills my bosom to thy tempered rays,
More fair than radiant smiles in beauty's keeping
   Through all the quiet of thy golden days
   Lie all things mantled in a dreamy haze —
Like wearied bosom in its tranquil sleeping,
Like gentle calm that cometh after weeping:
   Thine are the loveliest days.

They tell us of a far-off sunny clime
With noontide sheen on tropic splendors lying,
   Where all the year is one long blooming-time —
   Where song of Flora, in her joy and prime.
Wakes minstrel Echo with a joy replying
From morning's dawning until vesper's sighing,
     Through all the charmèd time.

Thy light, o'erlying all the azure wall,
So softly mellowed in its peerless shining;
   Thy sober-kindling sunshine over all,
   That lingers even where the shadows fall;
Thy frosted wreath, the vernal season's twining;
Thy faded scrolls, thine own fond first love's lining —
     These do surpass them all.

See yonder up what goodly altitudes!
Supremer heights, more tranquil airs, unveiling,
   Along the hills a purple glory broods;
   In all the silence of the Autumn woods —
A royal robe of tinted splendor trailing
O'er shrub and tree, unto rare beauty paling —
     A subtle spirit broods,

Like smile that trembles in Love's sorrowing tear;
Like fond regret some tender thought suffusing;
  Like heart high throbbing with a wealth of cheer,
  Though known of grief, nor stranger unto fear,
Though lone and saddened, yet in hopeful musing,
When some high faith hath recompensed its losing
      ·With well-enduring cheer.

  Though stilled the chorus of the choral throng,
More red than mountain peaks that sunset umbers
  Lies all the grove, late clamorous with song;
  A sacred calm these forest aisles along.
A holy hush, a Sabbath quiet slumbers;
A silent music breathes in mystic numbers,
      Sweeter than any song.

  I lowly listen to each Dryad rune,
Through lonely woodland haunts ecstatic straying,
  While all day long is one long afternoon:
  Had Eden fairer sublunary boon
Than Nature ever at this height delaying? —
Such rainbow-tinted sundowns her arraying,
      Gorgeous, at highest noon.

Brief are thy halcyon days, and fleeting fast.
Though yet October's milder reign imposing,
  As though thy hour most beauteous were last;
  Like faithful spirit, when its strife is passed,
In bosom of a deathless hope reposing:
So may my days, when hastening to their closing,
  Grow brighter till the last.

GARNERED SHEAVES.

When passed life's Summer days of heat and toil,
  As musing lone I sit with frosted locks,
  When passed the Passions' stormy equinox
And vain Ambition's labor and turmoil,
May I, O Autumn, bound with withered leaves
  And faded flowers that failed of ripened seeds,
Like thee, like thee count o'er my wealth of sheaves
  And harvest-hoard — the fruit of noble deeds.
Serene as falls thy light on amber slope,
  And woodlands far aflame like set of sun,
My failing days be beautiful with Hope;
And bear, like thine, my heart's wild yearnings stilled,
  The blest fruition of a labor done —
The glory of a destiny fulfilled.

WINTER LAYS.

THE bristling woods are tipped with gold,
  As dusky twilight shadows fall;
  I hear again the shepherd's call,
The sheep-bell tinkling to the fold;
The hearth-fire crackles to the cold,
  And faintly flickers on the wall.

Re-pile the grate, and spread the board,
  With little store, or plenty, blest:
  Still from thy larder bring the best;
Unlock the orchard's harvest hoard —
Whatever good thy hand hath stored:
  Then bid thy friend a welcome guest.

And while the slowly kindling blaze
  Leaps sparkling from the crackling fire,
  Bring forth the harp, attune the lyre,
And wake the songs of other days;
Love's olden long-forgotten lays,
  That win the soul to new desire.

And heart to heart, as eye to eye,
   Charm the slow-winging hours away
   With tales of many a vanished day
And severed link and sundered tie;
Of loved ones dead, that never die,
   And other near ones, far away.

Or join awhile the joyous train,
   And feel the pulses dance and leap
   Where merry feet in mazes sweep
Unto the viol's mellow strain;
While moonlight silvers o'er the plain,
   And starry eyes their watches keep.

Look where yon ice-bound river winds
   Afar the cragged hills between:
   See high above its snowy sheen
The glimmer of a thousand pines,
That all the dim horizon binds —
   A massy belt of living green.

Deep rooted in the soilless earth
   See heavenward rear their giant forms,
   Though scarce the glow of Summer warms
Those serried steeps of frost and dearth;
Mid rocks and barrenness their birth,
   High cradled by the eddying storms.

And so the soul, in soil of care,
  On glaring glacier peaks of woe,
  Shall like yon pines amid the snow
A fadeless wreath of beauty wear —
Be brighter for the frosty air,
  And stronger for the winds that blow.

THE night-winds sigh along the sedge;
  While on the orient's silver crest
  The thickly sombering shadows rest;
High, pile on pile, a beetling ledge
Seems toppling on the horizon's edge,
  Of clouds upgathering in the west.

Where Autumn shed his sober light
  O'er shining fields of golden grain,
  Whence blended in one glad refrain
Came harvest songs of home delight,
We see, alas! but dearth and blight,
  And hear the storm shriek out amain.

The sable gloom the morning wears
  Chill o'er the orient's misty bar,
  The clouded noon, so dim and far,
But type the heart my bosom bears:
O'ershadowed by a thousand cares,
  And rayless of each heavenly star.

Yet soon the onward rolling year
    Shall bring again each vanished day —
    Spring shed a warm and joyous ray
Adown the vale now lone and drear;
New leaf in green the forest sere,
    And robe the hills in bloom of May.

So may our souls, though all unblest,
    And bowed in sorrow overlong,
    With olden Summer glories throng;
And feeling's most divine unrest
Full flood again the empty breast,
    And brim the crystal wells of song.

The cones that pierce yon purple light
    Have seen a hundred winters flee,
    And other hundred years shall see;
Ere, yielding to the tempest's might,
They topple from their dizzy height,
    My simple harp will cease to be.

Yet will I tune my wintry lyre,
    Though it may wake no note of fame,
    To nobler purpose, higher aim,
To feel each wingèd thought aspire;
While brighter glows the kindling fire,
    And still more bright the social flame.

So will I cheer the hour with song;
　　Nor doubt along life's darkened ways
　　There swells some echo of my lays
In hearts where mystic murmurs throng;
More sweet, if love the strain prolong,
　　Than hollow trumpet-tongue of praise.

ALL day the forest oaks have swayed
　　Their branches with a restless sweep;
　　The winds their stormy revels keep
Through wooded wilds, in field and glade;
While round the cotter's hut delayed
　　Still higher piles the drifting heap.

All day upon my heart has lain
　　The shadow of a nameless fear;
　　I stay the overbrimming tear,
And still my bosom's throb of pain;
But its disquiet comes again,
　　And deepens as the glooms appear.

No vain regret for loved ones dead
　　Lives in this strangely-aching smart;
　　Nor careless hand with ruthless dart
Anew some olden wound hath bled;
Nor know I whence the sorrow dread
　　That casts its shadow on my heart.

And is there by the soul possessed
   A chord that feels prophetic thrill,
   Presaging grief erewhile to fill
The coming time with sore unrest?
A horoscope within the breast,
   And this its dark portent of ill? —

Some Stormy Petrel's warning cry
   On Life's lone seas? — the haunting wraith
   Of yet uncoffined love and faith?
The twanging of a sundered tie?
The kiss of lips that soon shall lie
   Mute in the miracle of Death?

Ah well! — of Truth the rarest seeds
   Are sorrow-sown; from out the dust
   Our tears have wet — the wreck and rust
Of perished hopes and buried creeds,
Spring harvests new of nobler deeds
   Of purer love and higher trust.

———

FULL many a day the biting snow
   Has cumbered wide the saddened plain:
   Still higher heaps the drifting lane,
Still bleak the storm-winged tempests blow:
We seek the sun's serener glow
   From out the burdened skies in vain.

The fleecy tenants of the fold
  Still mourn the meadow's grassy boon:
  The kine. the heathy copse to prune.
Lone wander on the dreary wold
And look, while shivering with the cold.
  For pity to the clouded moon.

Like yeanlings reft of mother's breast.
  That Summer's sunlight sadly miss.
  Or, bowed in wintry loneliness,
Like yonder kine, with hunger pressed.
I wander on Life's weary waste,
  Amid the blighted boughs of bliss.

———

O'ER leagues of snow-emmantled earth
  The Christmas bells are ringing clear;
  Thrice-welcome hour, though bleak and drear.
And harbinger of storm and dearth:
In loving smiles and glowing hearth
  Thou bringest more than Christmas cheer.

O hallowed day! to thee allied
  Is all that most this life endears
  Of faith and hope—of doubt and tears,
And love of One for love that died,
Yet lives again, and glorified
  In thee, through twice a thousand years!

To-day shall Absence and Regret
   Their iron sceptre yield to you;
   For friends to old affection true
Across the stormy years have met,
And eyes with joy's suffusion wet
   Drink light from kindred eyes anew.

To-day the sire that feebly bows
   Shall flush with seeming youth the while;
   And careless girlhood's happy smile
Re-light its glow on matron brows;
While blissful dreams and loving vows
   Shall many a maiden care beguile.

To-day shall grief, in anguish prone,
   From pain a respite gladly win;
   And he who owns no bosom-kin,
Who threads Time's wintry maze alone.
Shall start at oft-endearing tone—
   Brief murmur from the life within;

And musing sad, his heart shall lean
   To olden memories, hope-embossed;
   The latest loved, the early lost,
Perchance are with him, all unseen,
From Paradise of summer-green,
   To soothe his spirit, tempest-tossed;

Or on his deeply visioned eye
    Rise fairest forms we may not see—
    Loom other landscapes, blooming free;
As, with a trust that may not die,
He ponders long each sundered tie,
    Or bond more beautiful to be.

———

THE mist lies heavy on the hills,
    And shrouds in gloom each rocky steep;
    The dusky clouds above them sleep.
Whence slow the trickling rain distils.
Like some o'erburdened lid that fills
    With gathering tears it can but weep.

The fleecy snow and glistening rime
    Are melting from the earth away;
    I look upon her mantle gray,
And think me of the blooming-time,
And mark the day-god slowly climb
    Still higher up the walks of day.

And glad to know each vanished storm
    Will go to grace the Summer hour,
    And add new beauty to the bower
That drinks the sunshine glad and warm,
And give each fairy floral form
    A greener leaf and gayer flower.

So oft the troubled heart must know
  The binding of an icy chain;
  Yet dewy tears, like Summer rain,
Shall bid the frigid fountain flow —
Life wear anew its vernal glow,
  And feeling's pulses leap again.

Some long-forgotten voice may wake
  The murmur of an early song;
  Or secret echo, silent long,
A well-remembered music make;
And oh! the aching heart must break,
  Or tears dissolve each icy thong.

So shall we win from all things here
  A trust for good in everything,
  And hear Hope's bright-winged songsters sing
Behind the wintry clouds of fear;
And know, when watered by a tear,
  Love wears anew the flush of Spring.

BY THE FIRESIDE.

DEEP in the forest brown and bare
   I hear the Genius of the Storm;
   I see the outline of his form
Dark pictured on the frosty air;
And mid the tall oaks waving there,
   The swaying of his mighty arm.

Though bleak the bitter winds that blow,
   And darkens on a dreary night,
   The wide hearth beckons warm and bright;
In converse sweet, in genial glow
Of Summers buried long ago,
   Is more than Summer's lost delight.

Awhile beside the cheerful blaze,
   Some story of the vanished time,
   And sweeter than the vesper-chime,
Come read me, dear; or lowly lays
From out the old heroic days,
   Of love through sorrow made sublime.
      *   *   *

Bring for our darling ones' delight
    Arabia's fairy wonder-tome,
    Or with the world-wide Pilgrim roam:
Tilt with the mad Castilian Knight;
Or look with Crusoe's yearning sight
    On seas that gird his Island Home.

Turn to the Ploughman-Poet dear:
    Let "Twa Dogs" wise their converse keep;
    With "Halloween" our pulses leap:
Bend o'er the "Mountain Daisy's" bier;
Sing "Bonny Doon;"—one tender tear
    With him for Highland Mary weep.

Read—of the Oak that lightly flung
    Abroad such wealth of songful lore
To lovers dear; or, turning o'er,
Of Alice, and the Bard that sung—
Albeit his heart with sorrow wrung—
    "That loss but made us love the more."

Of her whose breath passed in the sigh—
    "Sweet is true love, though given in vain;"
    Or her that, pierced with pity's pain,
Alone "clothed on with chastity,"
Rode at high noon through Coventry—
    Unrobed, yet without blame or stain.

17

Of him that with his Hermia strayed,
　　Slept a true lover and true knight;
　　On whom before the morning light
The Elfin's wizard charm was laid,
So, waking, he mistook the maid,
　　And broke, and lightly proffered, plight.

Is theirs alone the woe in weal?
　　Alas! such lovers all are we;
　　Where grows the herb whose potency
May, counter-charmed, our eyes unseal?
And each to each in truth reveal,
　　And this confusion cease to be?

Of her Wyoming darkly mourned —·
　　The maiden beautiful, that fell
　　By the red hand of war;—ah, well!
Precious the bliss her heart inurned
That said: "'T is Waldegrave's self," returned
　　Again —" of Waldegrave come to tell."

Of her that bore too long the smart
　　Of love delayed, yet keeping green
　　Love's lilies for the one unseen,
Counselling but her woman's heart,
Chose in all ways life's better part; —
　　Arcadian Evangeline.

Or, in the changeful Seasons, fly
  With Damon to the sylvan shade:
  Look on the foam-emmantled maid—
Behold love's sacred mystery!
Oh, for the lover's chastened eye
  To see all beauty, disarrayed!

Or roam Palemon's Harvest-land:
  There with the lowly damsel glean,
  And dream that Virtue's garments mean
Are Virtue's still; Love's sacred band
Is more than gold; that Beauty's wand
  Still, chastened, holds its sway serene.

Weep—buried in Lavinia's grave—
  For wedded loves in simple ways
  Of Nature, crowned with length of days,
And fairest treasures Hymen gave;
When "numerous offspring," sturdy, brave,
  And "lovely like themselves," was praise.
           *   *   *
Or turning, read in lowly tales
  And waifs of old idyllic song,
  Of weary hearts that suffered long,
Yet firm in trust that never fails;
For much their triumph us avails
  To make our faith in Virtue strong.

Of him that, far years gazing through,
    Looked on his Annie's face beside
    An alien hearth: then, sorely tried,
With yearning heart so tender-true,
Back into sheltering darkness drew,
    And held his purpose till he died.

Of him, the Chief of Table Round,
    That bore the matchless cimeter—
    The mystic brand Excalibur;
Great Arthur! he the Blameless crowned:
That in such pitying grief profound
    Bent o'er his erring Guinevere.

And is there other sorrow—care
    So infinite, supremely great
    As theirs, alas! who yearning wait
Prone by a darkened hearth, and bear
To Love an agonizing prayer
    For love that, wandering, lingers late?

Of him, the pride of Ithaca:
    The greatest his of names that throng
    Heroic annals; brave and strong—
Mighty for noble deeds!—may we,
Like him, the Island Charmer flee,
    Nor harken to the Sirens' Song.

Of him who, Lethe's waters passed,
    In Hades journeyed far below —
    Dark mapped the nether realms of woe;
Thence rising to Elysian rest,
Saw all the legions of the blest
    Whose garments are as drifting snow.

But turn the visioned tome with awe;
    For who so pure to taste the bliss
    Of Dante and of Beatrice?
Yet owning still the primal law,
All hearts do inspiration draw,
    O Woman, from thy loveliness!
            *   *   *

Lo, Midnight lingers at the gate!
    Still wide the lettered page unrolls
    Where Fame heroic deeds enscrolls:
And oft returning shall we wait
Around the hearthstone, conning late
    These chronicles of noble souls.

And though the world do doubt their sooth,
    And sceptic's scoff be on him cast
    Who counts such legends of the Past
More than a fabled dream of youth,
Yet will we trust their very truth —
    Or strive to make them true at last.

MISCELLANEOUS.

Ever the Moon the Sea draws on apace;
  Earth trembles, swaying unto orb afar;
  No star but turning unto answering star,
Kindles and burns unto remotest space;
          Orion's flaming car
Draws all the Hosts of heaven—a shining train;
  So in thy wider realm, O world of Mind!
A fine electric tie—lore's mystic chain
  Doth kindred Spirits bind.

SONGS OF THE TOILER.

THE Seasons as they come and go—
  Spring's gentle sunshine warm,
The Summer's heat, the Autumn's glow,
  The Winter's cloud and storm;
The flowers that drink the dews of morn
  The earth-bescreening sod,
The myriad forms of beauty born
  In the wide realms of God;
The rivers as they seaward wend,
  The sea-waves' wild turmoil,
The winds the sturdy forest bend,—
  Are the High Priests of Toil.

18

They who in lettered lore untaught,
   Yet deeper visioned be.
Who read, in Sibyl-cipher wrought,
   In earth and air and sea
The good Beneficence intends,
   In sun and dew and rain
See Nature working to vast ends
   Through all her fair domain, —
Shall feel their life at one with these,
   Nor from their task recoil,
But leave the languid paths of Ease
   For the broad fields of Toil.

Joy to the Toiler! — him that tills
   The fields with Plenty crowned;
Him with the woodman's axe that thrills
   The wilderness profound;
Him that all day doth sweating bend
   In the fierce furnace heat;
And her whose cunning fingers tend
   On loom and spindle fleet!
A prayer more than the prayer of saint,
   A faith no fate can foil,
Lives in the heart that shall not faint
   In time-long task of Toil.

A bliss the sluggard never knows
    Deep in his heart shall spring,
Whose life flows as the tide-wave flows —
    Creation's antheming!
Whom ceaseless din of labor charms
    Like new-world's primal song;
As grow his swart and sinewy arms,
    His soul grows free and strong;
Till over all a glory springs
    On mine and mill and soil,
And the stern destiny that brings
    A heritage of Toil.

PEACE to the troubled years agone!
    Their darkest day is set,
Though round the ages' rosy dawn
    The shadows linger yet;
Full many a wondrous work is wrought,
    More wondrous yet to be
Than flashing of undying Thought
    Across the unfathomed sea:
And lo! the mystery that sleeps
    In Magian Serpent's coil —
The lightnings in the vasty deeps
    Chained to the car of Toil!

Still endless weave the subtle band
    O'er ocean, vale, and hill,
Till far to one electric hand
    Shall million pulses thrill!
O God, this old world never knew
    Such prophecy of Peace!
More faith and love our wrongs subdue,
    With light our hopes increase;
Revealing near, like morning sun,
    Above the Past's turmoil,
Our hearts' wild dream Utopian —
    A Brotherhood of Toil!

What time the noble Worker-band —
    The true, the free. the bold,
With swarthy brow and bony hand,
    Like warrior host of old,
From where the Southern sunlight shines.
    Or Mississippi glides,
Lone ceaseless sing our Northern pines,
    Wild break Atlantic tides, —
From many a land afar shall come,
    And not to feud and broil;
But to the festive Harvest-home
    And Carnival of Toil.

Roll up the full-orbed Freedom-star
   To light Earth's desert fields;
Affright the solitudes afar
   With sound of rolling wheels,
Thou fiery steed whose fearful neigh
   Wakes wide our sovereign Land!
Thou mighty triumph of To-day
   From Labor's cunning hand!
Thy argosies no storms betide,
   No tempest's wrath may spoil;
For all unheeding wind or tide,   .
   Thou tread'st thy path of Toil.

————

THE Giant Slave, that may not tire,
   But work the long day through
With thews of steel and lungs of fire,
   Has other task to do
Than delve the mine or rive the hill
   Or wind the furnace-glow,
Or drive the plane, the forge, the mill.—
   To plough and reap and sow!
Till none shall walk with aching feet,
   With weary trudge and droil,
But kingly proud, as seemeth meet
   The royal sons of Toil.

The mighty sinew-powers that wait
  In earth and sea and air,
Shall tireless early toil and late—
  Our menial burdens bear:
Their iron feet still fleeter flee—
  Our errands speed apace,
Till only Art and Science be
  The Helots of the Race!
The Toiler's glorious destiny
  No more to drudge and moil;
His labor loving labor be—
  Serene, untiring Toil.

Joy to the Toiler everywhere!
  Still let his hand be plied;
Wide plant the rose to blossom fair
  In many a desert wide;
A richer blessing year by year
  Win from old mother Earth;
A purer household altar rear
  By the endearing hearth;
Let wiser Thought to Labor given
  Redeem lost Eden's soil;
Then fair shall bloom the Flowers of Heaven
  In the sweet Homes of Toil.

TANNHÄUSER.

ALL our modern skies are clouded with a sceptic gloom
and haze—
With the dust of vanished years;
Though the paling stars are shining, they have lost
their mystic chime,
Singing to our duller ears;—
So the ancient myths and legends, stories of the Olden
Time,
That the fading Past endears,
Only to the eye that reads them by the light of other
days,
Are instinct with Truth sublime.

Yet to-day by cottage firesides still, by mountain, moor,
    and fell,
    As in far-off Aryan times,
Lives the Folk-Lore of the Ages;—are by wrinkled
    grandames told
    All the nursery tales and rhymes:
Faithful John and Cinderella, he the Master Thief and
    bold —
    Stories of all lands and climes;
Famous sleepers, wondrous pipers, matchless archers;—
    and they tell
    This among the legends old:
      *   *   *

In a mountain of Thuringia, where the storms their
    revels keep,
    Hidden in its heart of rock,
Is the dwelling of Frau Holda, where her worshippers
    resort,
    Is the famous Horselloch:
Whence is heard the cry of anguish and the laugh of
    demon sport —
    Frenzied tongues that jeer and mock
Blent with sound of angry billows in some dread abys-
    mal deep, —
    Cave where Venus holds her court.

Only simple souls and lowly have the gift of clearer
    sight —
Have that rarer vision won;
To the lone belated peasant, as he weary homeward
    strode,
    Plodding slow at set of sun,
Oft that terror-haunted Venusberg a sudden wonder
    showed;
    Brightening all the shadows dun,
Saw he shining forms of maidens dancing in the spec-
    tral light —
    Dwellers in that weird abode.

And the valiant knight, Tannhäuser, he, the troubadour
    renowned,
    To all bold adventures led.
With his great heart sole companioned, journeying late
    but unafraid
    By that cavern yawning dread,
Saw uprising thence resplendent in the twilight's falling
    shade
    One of queenly form and tread;
And she beckoned to him smiling, with her cestus-zone
    unbound,
    In all loveliness arrayed.

19

As with kindling eye and eager feet he climbed that
                        perilled way,
        Lo! before him watching late
Rose an old man, Faithful Eckhardt—there with white
                staff doomed to stand,
        Warn and ward from evil fate;
The fore-herald when at midnight ride the Wild Hosts
                through the land;
        And he looked with pity great
On that gallant minnesinger, lured by beauty's phantom
                        ray,
        And he waved a warning hand.

But in vain: Tannhäuser gazing on that unveiled glory
                        near,
        In its wizard charm and thrall,
Saw not him, the faithful warden, nor the hand high
                waved in air;—
        Honor, fame, gold, comrades—all
Were but foregone things forgotten; saw he but that
                vision fair.
        Heard he but that Siren-call;
Music more than harp of Orpheus to his enchanted
                        ear,
        Drowned that omen-tongued " Beware!"

On his good steed, on the outer world one longing look
  he fed —
 To that Goddess turned, and lo!
Far she drew him to her palace, lit and garnished gor-
  geously,
  In the mountain far below;
And the hours went by unheeded, from all thought but
  pleasure free,
  And the wine-cups overflow;
Wild delights and bacchanalian, to all lustful pleasures
  wed,
  Rioting and revelry.

Nymphs with floating tresses shining like the gold in
  sunset sky,
  Waked the love-enchanted lyre;
And each hot erratic passion in his fiery soul
  intense.
  Kindled into fierce desire;
All delights that beauty wanton, clasped in rapt delirious
  dance,
  And the foaming bowl inspire,
Freely quaffed he — until seven years had fled unheeded
  by;
  All the ravished joys of sense.

But ere long the soul that slumbers with remorse shall
    stricken be—
Must each sin its sorrow bear;
And Tannhäuser, again longing for the sunshine's
    clearer ray,
For a breath of purer air,
Cried unto the Virgin Mother, though with lips unused
    to pray,
In his anguish and despair:
She, with tender heart of pity, set his erring footsteps
    free
In the light of upper day.

More than jewelled halls and joy of wine and ribald jest
    and song
In the caverns underground,
Was to him the sun new-risen, was the dew-besprinkled
    sod,
Was the streamlet's leap and bound;
Was the path of mountain-chamois, that his foretime
    footsteps trod,
Was the sheep-bell's tinkling sound;
And his soul, that wakened conscience sore reproved of
    sin and wrong,
Longed to be at peace with God.

But in vain his crimes confessing. he could no remission
find.
Though priest after priest he sought:
Still he wandered, sore benighted, in the unabated
gloom
Of his evil-darkened thought;
Humbly to the Pope he bowed him: he could not unseal
the doom
Of such condemnation wrought:
Sooner should the staff that bore him, like a garland
summer-twined,
Bud and quicken into bloom.

Then, a darkened soul unshriven through the endless
years to bear,
Bowed in sorrow, doubt, and pain,
Turned he from the world of sunlight—his great heart
with anguish torn,
To that Venusberg again. . . . .
Three days. and behold! the Father's staff had—pass-
ing wonder!—borne
Buds and blossoms; but in vain;
For still he for whom no priestly hand might absolution
dare
Must his sin unpardoned mourn.

Quick with awe arose Pope Urban—rode his messengers
        amain;
    And they sought the Horsel vale;
Late—alas! too late! . . . . . How oft too late our hearts
        forgiveness bear! . . . .
    Far along the mountain trail
A lone, wayworn, haggard man had passed, with weary
        feet of care—
    Passed with troubled brow and pale;
Since, Tannhäuser has been seen no more;—nor home-
        returning swain
    Since has seen that Goddess fair.
            *   *   *

And is this my homely legend but a story of the
        Past?
    Or the Present all unguessed?
Of some mighty Truth dishonored by its prophet over-
        bold—
    By its false evangelist?
And our souls the lost Tannhäuser, seeking vain, with
        grief untold,
    The One Faith of peace and rest;
Till unto their painted idols they despairing turn
        at last—
    Gods of Pleasure, Fame, or Gold?

REVISITED.

DOWN - FALLEN, the Trojan's grand
Renowned ancestral halls
The far world mourned; and her, Persepolis,
With all her loveliness,
And Carthage — touched as by a wizard wand;
And still with grief recalls
Rome, Albion, aglow,
The Crescent's shrines laid low,
And her that stood where Moscow's temples stand.

But what are these to me?
They lighten, pale, and show
Like far-off flaring of a furnace-blast —
A pageant of the Past,
Fearful and grand, flaming in History!
With thee it is not so,
Belovèd, thee I knew
While yet thy days were few,
And all thy greatness in the time to be.

As oft to ripened years
        Some youth and maid unknown
Together grow from childhood's summers brief,
        Till one in joy or grief
That evermore them each to each endears,
        Have we together grown;
        But oh! as he that goes.
        Whose fond heart thrills and glows,
Hiding the pain of love's delicious fears, —

Joyous, and bearing thence
        Treasured affections old,
Lit with the brightness of one form and face, —
        Returning, finds each grace
And beauty withered by the pestilence,
        Sad weeping unconsoled,
        Deplores and mourns in vain:
        Such is my bosom-pain,
Finding in all my loss no recompense.

In anguish prone I wait
        Where ruins strew the plains —
Where smoldering heaps the wealth-bethronging mart
        By fallen shrines of Art,
Oblivioned tomes, and hearthstones desolate;

Religion's fallen fanes,
And Learning's halls o'erthrown;
By trees stripped, blackened, lone,
Dead — monuments of a relentless Fate!

Oh, who can paint the gloom —
The woe that on thee fell,
When onward bore the fright-bewildered throng,
A hundred thousand strong!
Forlorn, and fleeing from a fiery doom,
As from the flames of Hell!
Treasures that toil had wrought —
Treasures of gold unbought,
Buried in indistinguishable tomb!

And how aghast and dumb
We stood, when from the Pit
Vile demons rose; bore high with maniac hand
The all-devouring brand!
With pillage, hate, — fell brood of lust and rum —
More wide thy horror lit;
As if foul fiends, accursed
Of God and man, had burst
The fiery gates of Pandemonium!

20

We hark the bell that tolls
          Thy fallen fame—but tongue
Can never tell thy tale of miseries,
          Of awful tragedies;
Of martyrdoms no poet's pen enrolls;
          Of noble deeds unsung;
          Of thy uncoffined dead;
          Thy living hosts that tread
Serene the heights, with all heroic souls!

As unto her that grieves
          Less for her pain than his,
The lover's—he, alas! who can but miss
          Her dower of loveliness—
Our pity yearns, and quick each want relieves
          With thousand charities;
          Brings for love's deeper needs
          Kind words and gentle deeds,
And thus, in little part, her loss retrieves:—

So, with one heart amain,
          In tender sympathies,
To thee the people of all tongues and lands
          Have stretched full, pitying hands:
Anon have sought to soothe thy poignant pain

With all sweet ministries;
Until our souls go out
To ask, not all in doubt,
If in this fiery wrath be more of loss or gain.

Can aught again restore
The old-time beauty?   No.
Ah, me!   Howbeit, the soul that fair arrayed
In every grace the maid,
Still lives as when those outward charms it wore;
And Love, bewailing so,
Beholding how of pain
Is wrought the spirit's gain,
At length is comforted, and weeps no more.

And thou that wert so fair,
And now low in the dust,
Bearing thy weight of grief—thy grime and stain,
Without complaint of pain;
With hands still quick to do, as heart to dare—
Strong in all toil and trust;
I see thee, sorely tried,
Uprising purified,
And hope again is born of my despair.

Shall not the near years show
        Thee crowned and lovely—nay,
Fairer than in thy maiden beauty brief?
        And we, erelong our grief
Outworn—what time the harvest sheaves of woe
    We reap—shall we not say,
        Recalling without pain
        Our anguish, "then in vain
We wept and mourned—but it was better so"?

    Alas! we only see
        Dimly—and darkly spell
In pain and loss, above all cant or creed
        Sermons we can but heed;
Oh, for the faith that One, whatever be,
        Doth order all things well!
        We feel—we do not know—
        It somehow must be so:
Our loss be still thy gain, Humanity!

MINE OWN.

THOU who turnest, sore and fainting,
    From life's discord, clang, and jar,
        Weary longing for thine own, —
Like a bird its sorrow plainting,
        Singing lone
     In the wilderness afar; —
Spirit that with mine is waiting
        Spirit-mating,
   Kindled at a kindred star; —

O Beloved! that didst lighten
    To my childhood — that didst show
      Like a beacon far away,
And that evermore didst brighten
        Day by day
    With my youth's intenser glow,
Still the dreams of an aspiring
       Manhood firing,
   Thou dost more a beauty grow.

And a deeper joy divining:
    Though we wander wide apart.
        Seeking vain love's peace and rest.
Oft I feel thy arms entwining —
    In my breast
    Feel the throbbing of thy heart;
And I see in all transcendent
        Forms resplendent —
See the loveliness thou art.

Nature. smiling, ever drew me,
    As if hiding thee, my bride;
        Garlanded with graces rare,
Thee the lilies show unto me,
        Passing fair;
    Thee the violets bashful hide;
And the rose, all sweets inurning,
        Crimson burning,
With thy blushes. love. is dyed.

Oft I see thee darkly, dwelling
    In the Spring-time's greenery;
        In the Summer's anthem-song
Love soft murmurs, of thee telling
    All day long —

Charms the night's serenity;
Wakes in orison and idyl.
        Hymn and bridal
Of the woodland minstrelsy.

And thy heart is beauty-haunted:
    Thou, thy fainting bosom fanned
        With a breath from Eden-climes,
Too dost tread the realm enchanted; —
        Hark the chimes
    From that far celestial land!
Thrilling to the fervid grasping,
        Hallowed clasping
Of a dear love-plighted hand.

Hope, unto the new day turning,
        Plumes her joy-empurpled wings,
    Far outsoaring ill and strife;
Or to charm the maiden, yearning
        To the wife,
    At Love's altar sits and sings
Of two lives to one inblending —
        Still ascending,
    Soaring unto higher things.

And some gleam perchance just stealing
Faintly on life's widening skies,
That with mystic glory shine.
Kindles like the dawn, revealing —
Bliss divine! —
Baby lips and cherub eyes;
Half disclosing and yet hiding
Joys abiding
From a sinless paradise.

· Dost thou startle at the vision?
And why not thou, darling, find
Love's high destiny and good?
Realize the dream elysian —
Motherhood —
In thy woman's breast enshrined;
The one marvel of all story.
The one glory,
The one crown of Womankind.

Yet through weary paths and lonely,
And with brambles overgrown,
Should we wander wide apart,
Finding each the other only
In a heart

Beating loyal to its own;
Though we wait as we have waited—
    All unmated
.   Tread the wide, wide world alone;—

O Belovèd! undespairing,
    Let our faith be strong to win;—
        Life is brief, but Love is long!
All the ills the trouble-bearing
        Ages throng,
    Error, anguish, wrong, and sin,
Shall not lovers leal dissever—
        Part forever
    Those who are the true-akin.

Let Time bar our souls asunder;
    Let the years be sorrow-sown;
        Let all meaner joys depart;—
In Love's bright imperial Yonder,
        Heart to heart
    I shall clasp thee, dear Unknown!
Every charm and grace arrayed in,
        Peerless maiden,
    I shall come unto MINE OWN!

IDLE HOURS.

METHOUGHT I had been idle all the day:
The plough was standing in the furrowed ground.
The sickle hanging where the sheaf was bound;
    While listless basking in the Summer ray,
Soft-tempered by o'erarching boughs that hung
In fragrant tassels where the violets sprung,
    The daylight's golden sands had run away.
    Yet now with joy I see, in after time,
That much was won in that unnoted hour:
The treasures of the world of thought and power—
    The chastened beauty of the true sublime—
The ceaseless plodding worldling never finds;
For only in a tranquil moment binds
    The spell that wakes the Minstrel's mystic chime.

WAITED FOR.

SPRING's darling blossoms in their loamy prison
   Sleeping in tiny buds beneath the snow,
   Though darkly buried in the mould below,
Feeling the warmth of fervid suns unrisen,
   They, yearning, throb and glow:
So, dearest, hidden from all outward seeing,
   My heart fore-felt thy love, until it grew
A conscious presence to my inner being
   Ere yet thy form I knew.

As oft, while yet the chilling glooms encumber,
   We feel the breath of Summer days to be,
   So was it, love, when first I looked on thee;
My soul leaped up — breaking its icy slumber —
   O fateful prophecy!
As when we hear the early partridge drumming,
   Or the first cuckoo on the hills away,
Thrilling, it cried — " Surely the Spring is coming,
   And cannot long delay."

And now are overpassed the wintry shadows;
  Now all about us is the balmy air
  Of orchards reddening in the May-day fair;
And like to fragrant groves and thymy meadows
    The hearts our bosoms bear;
Dreaming sweet dreams, dear as the dreams of heaven.
    Singing love's old immortal rapture-rune;
Like bees late drowsing in the flowers at even,
    Droning a blissful tune.

O peace and rest! what after long delaying
  Is to the thirsty earth the copious rain,
  Love is to aching heart and tired brain;
Time's barren waste, to vernal impulse swaying,
    Fresh-verdured, smiles again;
The quickened fields afar, soft-greening, brighten;
    In the new day the mountains stand impearled:
A sun new-risen, a new world to lighten —
    And ours that newer world.

O Love divine! in thy glad realm eternal
  Can ever be or pain or want or fear?
  Nay — we would hold this failing life too dear,
Flesh-habited. to taste the joy supernal
    Of thy transcendent sphere.

Yet seems this purer air a rapt inhaling,
   In little part, of the ethereal breath
From climes beyond—our outer senses failing—
   What blindly we call Death.

Deep in the bud, its beauty-dream confessing,
   There hides a glory and a mystery—
A promise of the fruitage yet to be:
So may love ripen into priceless blessing,
   Beloved, for thee and me;
Of blossoms withered, with hope buried lying
   In graves that vainly did my tears bedew.
May this new Summer of the heart, undying,
   All the lost bloom renew.

And when, albeit bearing the heat and burden
   Of the fierce noontide with its grime and moil,
   Wide sowing, haply into fallow soil,
The seeds of Truth—waiting the harvest-guerdon:
   For all the long day's toil
May each the other strengthen and embolden,
   In every high endeavor hand in hand;
Till in Life's field the ripened sheaves stand golden
   O'er all the Autumn-land.

UNDER THE OAKS.

O CALM retreat! O love-delighted bowers!
Where not alone the woodbine twines and blooms,
But all ideal beauty lights the glooms;
    Where Poesy—that inspiration dowers
And genius nurtures in the mind and heart,
Till grown to forms of high creative Art—
    Yields rare delight through all the tranquil hours,
    The happy idle hours! O moments blest!
O solitudes instinct with higher life
To medicine the soul—its care and strife,
    Its low desires, its prone world-weary quest,—
When in your sacred haunts of wood and glen
I respite seek from toil, oh yield again
    A joy beyond—those sweeter fruits of Rest!

UNANSWERED LETTERS.

As he that looks with longing eye
  Across the blue seas, tempest - tossed,
  Lone shipwrecked on a barren coast,
To see some hope - winged bark go by,
Or he the Stygian waters nigh —
   A wandering ghost,
May longing wait, and waiting tire, —
So do we watch, in vain desire,
  Day after day, an empty Post.

And sorely vexed with jealousy.
  We feed the vagrant thoughts that bring
  Love's unrequited smart and sting:
"My friend no longer cares for me;
An idle dream that we might see
   In anything
The self - same beauty — cease to mourn
A feeble friendship overworn,
  Nor nurse the faded flowers of Spring."

Or marvel if our last, missent,
 Still keeps its ardent message sealed;
 Or feeling's fervid page revealed
Some folly, though for wisdom meant;
Or sigh, " Alas, if love be spent
  Or hearts congealed!"
Howbeit, only this is known:
Our friendship's fairy garden grown,
 So all too soon, a barren field.

The while perchance our waiting friend,
 Grown sick with joy delayed, nor gets
 The long expected missive, frets:
"O love—our being's sum and end!
Why still these precious moments lend
  To vain regrets,
Or dream some other may be true?
No more shall life its faith renew
 In other men, if he forgets!

"O doubt that deepens more my woe!
 Had I the trust, undimmed of fears,
 That his the love Time but endears,
That burns with an unfailing glow,
How would I all this care forego—

This grief and tears!
To know his heart still all my own,
I in this darkened world alone
    Would wait content a thousand years."

So longing on we faint and tire:
 · And is this priceless good we wait —
    Some friend with every mood to mate.
But offspring of a vain desire?
Or love to which our souls aspire.
            Or soon or late
May yet our famished bosoms know?
Aye, nevermore to miss thee so.
    Companion of the heavenly state!

The gem the briny ocean urns
    Still bears, though hid, its ruby ray;
    Though storms enshroud the orb of day,
Behind the cloud the sunlight burns; —
Our friend, if true, still loves and yearns,
        Though far away;
And if our waiting hearts but keep
Their faith, a fuller joy shall heap
    The measure of love's long delay.

22

COMPENSATIONS

THE clime whose skies are ever clear
Through all the swiftly circling year,
Unknown to gloom of Winter drear,
 The ever-shading palm may show;
 And there the fig and olive grow,
 And spicy breezes gently blow,
And downy blooms do softly lie
On all things, charming sense and eye
 With Beauty's fadeless show.

But where through many a dreary day
The Frost King holds unyielding sway —
Where, far aslant, the beams of day
 With shining on the glittering snow
 Can wake no warm and kindling glow;
 Where storm above and storm below
Do darken o'er the saddened plain
With frosty mist or sleety rain
 Or cloud of drifting snow, —

There strength is found with wisdom wed,
The lightest foot, the firmest tread.
And there the truest hearts are bred;
 And there the earth in bounty rears
 The frugal corn's most golden ears,
 And there the wheaten sheaf appears;
There Plenty cumbers all the ground
With luscious fruits, the sweetest found;
 There Art her temple rears.

So hold thy way; in heart be strong,
Though evil hosts do round thee throng
Of sorrow, disappointment, wrong;
 These are the Winters of thy life,
 With hidden wealth of promise rife;—
 So shrink not from the peril-strife,
And Autumn's store shall yet be thine,
And Peace serenely on thee shine
 Through long bright Summer-life.

HOME.

How many a charm within the precinct lies
Of one's own home — all hid to stranger eyes;
   In every spot some beauty-shrine is reared —
In garden walk, though flower and bloom be flown,
In wildwood sacred haunt, though drear and lone;
Though sings chill Winter with a sorrow-tone
   Among the leafless branches sad and seared;
   Oh, whatso'er affection hath endeared,
     Embalmed in beauty lies.

How full the joy when each familiar scene,
In frosty robe or vernal mantle green,
   Takes form and semblance of our inner life;
When thrilling tones of melody and song
In gentle hearts for love and duty strong,
Swell high and free and gladsome all day long.
   Till stilled are throbbings of each hidden strife;
   While all the solemn night-time hours are rife
     With radiant thought and scene.

THE BEAUTIFUL.

ALL my life long have I harkened
To a voiceless melody —
To a subtle music fine;
Dimly, as in shadow darkened,
A divine
Peerless form afar I see,
That anon more nearly smiling,
Me beguiling,
Still forevermore doth flee.

Like the Summer charms adorning
Regal nature everywhere
In a fadeless tropic land,
Like the glory of the morning
Rising grand,
Oft it shineth passing fair;
When I reach a hand to grasp it,
Ere I clasp it
All again is empty air.

Yet in endless beauty-dreaming.
　　Do I bear a heart and mind
　　　　Haunted by that vision vain;
Turn I from each vanished seeming
　　　　Yet again
　　To that good I fail to find,
As a dying soul unshriven
　　　　To the heaven
　　Where all Perfectness is shrined.

I would bear of human sorrow
　　　　Every mortal pang and throe—
　　　　　　Ill and loss and pain and wrong—
Could my heart the solace borrow
　　　　　　That ere long,
　　As the swift years come and go,
I shall clasp, no more to sever—
　　　　Mine forever—
　　Thee. the Beautiful I know!

I would dare, like pilgrim hoary,
　　　　Summer's sun and Winter's rain,
　　　　　　Homeless, weary, woeful, wan,
With unsandalled feet and gory,
　　　　　　On and on.—

Recking not of bruise and blain,
To this Mecca that I ponder
    Would I wander
Over seas of trackless plain.

I would dive with heart undaunted
    To old Ocean's roaring caves —
        Storm - embillowed, terror - gloomed;
Fearless tread, though darkness - haunted,
        Dread - entombed,
    Earth's Gethsemane of graves; —
Aye! wherever I could find it,
        Hold and bind it,
    That my yearning spirit craves.

I would brave ensanguined battle
    On the reddest field of strife;
        For the conflict fierce arrayed,
Eager grasp the glittering metal,
        Undismayed
    In the hour with carnage rife;
Shrinking not from any daring,
        To thee bearing —
    More than lover, bride, or wife.

I would trace the fiery fountains
 Of Sahara's desert sand —
  All life's pulses fever-fed;
Climb the glaring glacier mountains,
  Looming dread
 O'er the Arctic's frozen land;
Track the homeless tides that moan on,
  Breaking lone on
 Chartless leagues of barren strand.

On from world to world a-winging,
  Where more mellow moonlight lies
   The more tranquil seas along;
Whither new-born stars are singing
  A new song,
 And more radiant suns uprise;
Unto constellations nightly
  Burning brightly
 In the depths of stranger skies; —

Roam the boundless ether meadows
 That the starry hosts adorn —
  Boundless as Eternity!
High above these twilight shadows
  Would I flee,

Out beyond this mortal bourne,—
Could I find the realm transcendent
   Where resplendent
Hides the Beautiful I mourn.

Vision vain!—why should I wander.
   Sore with penance, pain, and prayer,
      Bearing an immortal dream?
Well I know the Good I ponder—
      Darkly deem,
   Is not outward anywhere:
Only in the heavens supernal
      Far, eternal
   Dwells the One divinely fair.

23

MOTHERHOOD.

In Life's wondrous gardens grow
    Vestal lilies, snowy white;
Roses flushed with morning glow—
    Flowers, the loving heart's delight:
Lowly pansies blooming fair—
    Many a beauty's opening bud;
But the charms beyond compare,
    Crown thee, beauteous Motherhood!

Let my fevered lip be fanned
    By the breath of loveliness:
Let the tenderest maiden hand
    Clasp my own in dear caress;
Light a heaven with starry eyes;
    Still my heart, all unsubdued,
Bears its purest sacrifice
    Unto queenly Motherhood.

Blushing bosom, budding warm,
    Though it deepest rapture shed.
Ever wears its sweetest charm
    Pillowing dainty baby head; —
See, while honeyed lips express
    Softly their delicious food,
Tiny fingers fond caress
    Bounteous breast of Motherhood.

Heavenly look of cherub eyes —
    Fair, oh passing fair to see;
Angels, only in disguise,
    Though they know it less than we; —
Who from these may coldly turn,
    Nor with loftier love subdued,
Feel his quickened being yearn
    To thee, saintly Motherhood?

Thou who bear'st in virgin breast
    Happy heart unwed to care,
Joyous in its loving quest,
    Whom thy mirror counteth fair, —
Maiden, matron - life is thine,
    Thine for evil or for good;
Most in this thy virtues shine —
    Miracle of Motherhood!

THE IMAGE-BREAKER.

THOUGH hushed since Delphi's tragic doom
    Each mighty oracle's response,
    Though every magic shape that haunts
The dusk of intervening gloom
Be silent—nor the shrouding tomb
    Give answer to Love's yearning wants,—

Oh, spare those idols of the Past
    Whose lips are dumb, whose eyes are dim;
    Truth's diadem is not for him
That comes the fierce Iconoclast;
Who wakes the battle's stormy blast,
    Hears not the angels' choral hymn.

In any creed, no heart-full prayer
    To faithful devotee is lost;
    Though dread-engloomed, and error-crossed.
Whate'er doth fruits of mercy bear,
Is true;—for this each error spare,
    Nor heap a common holocaust.

The faith that lights the pilgrim's way
   To loving Heaven—though not for you
   Its truth, to him must needs be true:
The rose that newly blooms to-day
Is pencilled by the primal ray:
   The New is old—the Old is new.

And if thy path no longer lies
   Through spirit-haunts of moor and fen,—
   If, as of old to prophet ken,
To thee the hills of Canaan rise,
With broader fields and ampler skies,
   And peopled wide with holy men,—

Remember still in charity,
   Thy brother's need is not as thine;
   Or, conning deep each darker line,
You too may find the mystic key
To every ward of mystery,
   And see in all a Truth Divine.

TOO LATE.

To every wrong
Not one—unnumbered penalties belong;
We expiate
Our deed with painful penitential tears.
To find, too late,
Thick in the breast the old avengers throng;
Part of that wages dread—the after years'
Remembrances of wrong.

There came a youth
To me long days agone; in form uncouth.
His brow sun-tanned,
Home-spun his coat, his garments all adust,
His bony hand
Just from the plough; but with the sun of Truth
Full on a manly face, lit with the trust
And the great heart of youth.

And I recall
The words he spake;—if they have turned to gall.
Ah well-a-day!
We cannot always keep an equal mind;
What we should say,
Alas, too oft we leave unsaid, and all
We should not say—the careless words unkind—
In vain we would recall.

"They tell me, Sir,
That you a Poet are,—your songs do stir
The hearts of men:
I too have rhymes: if they be good or ill
I cannot ken;
And you will tell me—if I do not err—
If there be aught in these of poet skill
Or promise, noble Sir."

I made reply
Unto that ardent youth of purpose high,
In cold disdain:
"Of songs," I said, "the world has all too much;"
As counting vain
His proffered rhymes, I pushed them idly by;
Him grudged the little courtesy—if such—
Wherewith I made reply.

More cruel, said:
"Do you not see that men have need of bread?
Seek not to win
A good whereto the strongest strive in vain;
The path wherein
Our feet have trodden long, we easy tread;
Late from the farm, I see:—return again
Unto the farm," I said.

And what is fame
To the dull eye, cold heart, ignoble aim?—
That youthful brow.
While yet I spake, lit with a purpose true.—
I see it now—
Flashed through the tan a beam of living flame:
A blush of shame—but oh, a blush that grew
Into immortal Fame.

So late—so late,
To learn what is ignoble, what is great;
So slow to see
Thought built the world, must build the world anew;
The Poet, he
The re-creator is whom all things wait:—
Recalling oft that youth, that poet true,
I sigh, "Alas, too late!"

HOME FROM THE WAR.

July 4th, 1865.

THE round globe turns unto the sun;
    The woods in waiting reverence lean;
    The far rejoicing hills between,
        The rivers run;
The golden dawn and twilight dun
    Weave wide their Summer robe of green.

The earth is thick with beauty sown;
    The Seasons, as they onward wing,
    The promise still of plenty bring —
        Of harvests grown:
Though priceless wealth in these we own,
    To-day joy hath a deeper spring.

Through all the wide rejoicing land
    We give with eager hearts unbound
    Unto our heroes, laurel crowned,
        A loving hand;
That come, a scarred and noble band,
    From many a crimson field renowned.

And let the farthest minster-dome
    Loud clang a mighty greeting forth;
    Ring east and west, ring south and north
        A welcome home
To all whose fearless feet have clomb
    To radiant heights of truth and worth.

Yet not alone for wild alarms
    Of deadly conflict heard no more,
    The bugle's call, the cannon's roar,
        The clash of arms,—
Nor yet to clasp the manly forms
    That foremost in the battle bore;—

Nor yet alone for victory bought
    Where free the crimson current ran,
    Our hearts rejoice;—for love of man
        In deeds enwrought!
A fadeless iris, glory-fraught,
    That far shall coming ages span.

For this, our Nation's starry goal,
    Though reached through fiery martyrdom,
    For Freedom's lifeless form become
        A living soul!
That while the circling seasons roll,
    No more shall outraged Truth be dumb.

And for a lowly race arrayed
  In manhood's regal majesty,
  Their native cane-fields tilling free
    And unafraid;
For Peace with deep foundations laid
  In righteousness, and Liberty.

Though mourning still our patriots gone.
  This faith a nation's tears shall stay;
  From fields still red with battle fray
    Their feet withdrawn,
They climb the radiant hills of dawn,
  That beacon on the coming day.

BELOVED.

THY love to me—like gentle Summer rain
    Is the outpouring of thy love to me,
When full libations o'er the parched plain
    Shower copious and free.

Thy love to me—like the deep hidden springs
    That from the hills in cooling freshness burst.
More pure the wave its sparkling fountain brings
    To quench my spirit-thirst.

Thy love to me—like the soft mystic chime
    That murmurs to us in the twilight dim;
A voice glad singing of the coming time—
    My heart's perpetual hymn.

Thy love to me—like the meek stars that shine
    From the far-glowing galaxy of night:
Only the brightness of these orbs is mine—
    Those have an alien light.

Thy love to me—no full, deep joy like this,
   In the wild fervor that my heart hath known;
The large fulfilment of my dreams of bliss
      Through weary years and lone.

Thy love for me—still present though unseen;
   Though lengthening miles must long between us lie.
Nor time can part, nor distance intervene:
      I feel thee ever nigh.

And still more nigh, as still more wholly mine—
   I still more thine becoming day by day.
Until the sun shall undivided shine
      That lights our severed way.

WORK.

'TIS much to know in life our proper task,
Yet more to do, when well we know our work;
Into Life's harvest none are sent to shirk —
    Of others' toil the gifts of labor ask;
Why should I beg? — couldst give me all the wealth
    Of all the world, I might not hold it fast —
    I could but die a mendicant at last.
It is not mine, the gold I get by stealth:
    Only in doing may the arm grow strong,
The mind be strengthened in its own high thought;
And ours — ours only what our hands have wrought.
    The sole sure wages that to Toil belong.
Do then thy task, and trust the gods' decree,
That as thy work thy recompense shall be.

CHRISTINE.

Sing us, O lady fair—
Not when afar
Upon the stifled air
The world's great anthem peal on peal resounds—
A lowly song;—not mid the din and jar
Of the deep organ-swells that blend and pour
In one grand symphony
All waves of sound
From full orchestra borne, like billows' roar
When tempests lash the sea.

Sing us the simple lays,
Home-ballads, born
In the dim mythic days,
Of mountain, sea, and river, wood and fell;
The Folk-songs old, that never are outworn!
So to our children when the years shall wane,
At twilight-fall serene
Oft may we tell
Of the sweet Singer from across the main—
Of her, the fair Christine.

Sing us old waifs of song
From Runic-writ,
That to the scenes belong
Now far away — such as in years agone
Delighted homely labors — charmed and lit
The fagot-bearing woods of Wexio;
What time, with joyance rare,
At peep of dawn,
Arrayed in home-wrought kirtle thou didst go
Elate to Ljugby Fair.

Sing us of childhood's hour
That comes no more:
Of all the wondrous dower
Of aspirations high — the longings wild
To know, to be, to do, to sing and soar.
To climb unto a far-off shining goal,
When thou didst wander free,
A happy child,
On Smoland hills, and feed thy hungry soul
On Nature's minstrelsy.

Sing us of all things fair:
Sing us of Home!
Of hearts that nightly bear
Yearnings for one beloved beyond the sea,
Counting the days that weary wax and gloam:

Sing us of her who with love's subtle art
   Fore-kenned thy happier lot;
     Who tearfully,
Stilling the throbbing of the mother's heart,
   Said, " Go, but ask me not!"

   Sing us of Fatherland —
     O theme sublime!
   Some tale from out the grand
Old Scandinavian Eddas that do bear
   Lore from the ancient days—the first of Time!
Some Saga-song of mighty heroes dead!
   Of Vikings bold—of all
     To Norland dear,—
Of Thor, of Odin, Freya—all that tread
   Walhalla's shining hall!

   Sing us of Love—but nay!
     Not for our ears
   · Is that sweet minstrelsy,
So dear with all regret;—from lips like thine,
   That song melodious of the coming years,
Whose prelude murmurs in the lowliest breast,
   Would pierce us till we die;—
     O song divine!
Sing us of Hope, of Trust, all sweet unrest,—
   Saddest of all—good-bye.

LITTLE LINNIE.

Oft in grief's dread shadow straying,
  With a heart o'erbrimming full,
Have I mourned the swift decaying
  Of the loved and beautiful;
I have trod a pathway darkened,
  Trod it wearily and lone,
While I hearkened, vainly hearkened
  For a sweetly vanished tone;
But a calm came with the morrow
  To my bosom's heaving tide,
For I only dreamed of sorrow
  Till our Little Linnie died.

Though I vainly yearning, nightly
　　Woo thee from the realm of dreams,
Seek thy radiant footstep lightly
　　Wandering by the crystal streams,
See the lonely twilight darken,
　　All unlit of love's delight,
Though still evermore to hearken
　　For thy nevermore "good-night;"
By the deeper love I bore thee
　　Than all other love beside,
Though my grief may not restore thee,
　　Though our Little Linnie died;—

Though the ages may not claim thee
　　For this darkened earth again,
Though my waiting lip shall name thee
　　Long, and lovingly, in vain;
I shall clasp my little maiden
　　In all angel graces grown,
If the years, with sorrow laden,
　　Do but bear me to mine own;
Clasp again the early taken,
　　Latest loved, love's only pride,
To this lorn heart, hope forsaken
　　When our Little Linnie died.

The dear azure heaven is shrouded
  Of those orbs of tender blue,
Or my own, with mists beclouded,
  They have darkened to my view;
Yet in vain my sore repining,
  Howsoever that may be,
For if still undimmed their shining,
  They are turned away from me;
And no solace can I borrow
  From the days that darkly glide.
For my first, last, only sorrow,—
  When our Little Linnie died.

O! how can I live without thee?
  If no more to feel the twine
Of thy gentle arms about me,
  Or thy tiny hand in mine;
Still to miss thy soft caressing
  Through the darkened days to be,
For thou wast the rarest blessing
  From the angel-life to me.
Only in the heavens above me,
  Where the Beautiful abide,
Were there any more to love me
  When our Little Linnie died.

THE TIME TO BE.

THE shadows lengthen as the day
 Declines along the Hesper-rim;
 The night draws on — more faint and dim
Fades the last purple light to gray;
Yet starry hosts come out alway,
 To echo on Creation's hymn.

Creation's hymn — that first was sung
 On boundless waste of shapeless gloom,
 When out of Chaos' quickened womb
The earth to orbèd being sprung;
While other orbs with music rung,
 To see the new-born light illume.

And what though countless ages wane.
 The while the Lichen race appears;
 At length the mighty forest rears,
And wide outspreads the verdured plain
With luscious fruits and golden grain; —
 Man crowns at last the ripened years.

Though chill and frail the Summer wears,
　　Till into stormy Autumn passed,
　　The sleety rain, the wintry blast.
Are Nature's need that loss repairs;
And Spring returns with balmy airs
　　And charms more mellow than the last.

And shall alone in beauty grow
　　These grosser outer things we see,
　　And not our lives more lovely be
Throughout the years that come and go?
Their brightness wear no deeper glow,
　　What time the circling seasons flee?

Though, seeming like old Night to mock
　　All order and all laws' control,
　　Looms on the dark the dawning soul,
Yet shall the storm and earthquake shock
And lava-fires subdue the rock,
　　And make its orb and circle whole.

And mantling over vale and hill,
　　The green and tender blade shall spring;
　　The fragrant bowers rich fruitage bring;
Each higher type of life infill,
Till from the thought and from the will
　　Dies out each vile and creeping thing.

And Mind throughout an endless day
    Shall range a freer, ampler scope;
    With spectral fear and error cope —
Anon each ghostly phantom lay;
And roam in joyous noontide ray
    Through paths wherein we darkly grope.

The Inner Life shall know its need,
    And unto newer life be born;
    From skies our lesser hopes adorn
Shall fade in light each darkening creed,
As swift the misty shades recedé
    Along the radiant path of morn.

With purer faith that upward leads
    Forever toward the Great Unknown,
    The infant Man, to manhood grown,
Shall write at length the Creed of Creeds —
A liturgy of nobler deeds
    Than yet this warrior-world has known.

And other prophet-stars shall rise
    And shine along the Mythic Page
    That lives anew in every age,
Yet with the dying ages dies;
Wherein a deeper meaning lies,
    That ever waits the wiser Sage.

And thought shall find a fuller speech.
   And still to loftier thought attain.—
   And deeply-hidden truths made plain
More deeply hidden truths shall teach;
As gazing from some mountain reach
   We see yet higher heights to gain.

And they whom selfish passions bind,
   To gentler sympathy unknown,
   As more of good enamored grown,
Shall more of good in all things find,
And be more kind unto their kind,
   And each in each a brother own.

And Freedom, grown more free and bold,
   The whole wide world shall fearless tread;
   And Science far a glory shed—
Strange wonders in her light unfold;
While hearts now bound in lust of gold
   Be unto holiest missions wed.

And progress-cycles still shall roll,
   Still unto rarer ether speed;
   Till Faith from cumbering. Form be freed,
To see in all the living Soul;
Still pointing on the better goal,
   Outgrown each grosser symbol's need.

COUSIN CAROLINE.

Ere the spring-time's dewy splendor
    Of thy sunny life had passed,
On thy young hopes, budding tender
    Fell a breath of wintry blast;
And thy youth full early parted
    From its blissful promise, thine;
Thou hast left us, gentle-hearted,
    Fragile cousin Caroline.

With a heart untaught to murmur,
    Thou didst suffer—not in vain ;
Patient growing still, and firmer,
    With thy still increasing pain ;
Long and weary years of anguish
    Thou didst number, nor repine,
Meekly droop, and drooping languish,
    Lovely cousin Caroline.

26

Grief our troubled bosoms steeping,
　Oh ! it was a wintry day,
When thy spirit left us weeping
　O'er its tenement of clay!
Yet we may not now deplore thee,
　For life's better part is thine,
Where thy sister-angels bore thee,—
　Our sweet cousin Caroline.

When the frosty band shall lighten
　Binding hill, and vale and plain,
When the vernal hours shall brighten
　O'er the gladdened earth again,
Who shall watch the flower bulb starting,
　Who shall train the budding vine,
From its trellis wayward parting,
　For our cousin Caroline ?

Soon each floral gem so cherished,
　Sleeping in its snowy tomb,
That, like thee, in beauty perished,
　Shall renew its pride of bloom ;
Though thy watchful care to lend them
　Now can never more be thine,
We, with willing hand, will tend them
　For our cousin Caroline.

Though we mourn that gloom hath shrouded
   Friendship's jeweled diadem,
In celestial skies unclouded,
   Shines another glory-gem,
With a radiance unborrowed,
   With serene, untroubled shine ;
Thou hast found thy home unsorrowed,
   Suffering cousin Caroline.

Oft in happy hours and lonely
   We shall miss thy cheerful tone,
Lost one—lost ?—no, parted only,
   Knowing thou art still OUR OWN !
For thou wilt not cease to love us,
   While each radiant orb shall shine
In the starry heavens above us,
   Dearest cousin Caroline.

And our weary steps do hasten,
   Journeying to that brighter shore,
Where no sorrow comes to chasten,
   Chastened, thou hast gone before;
We shall there, our grief foregoing,
   In love's recognition twine,
Never doubting of our knowing
   Thee, our cousin Caroline.

PARTING FRIENDS.

When the chosen Friend, and dear,
Leaves us for some far-off land,
When unbid the falling tear
Glistens on the clasping hand;
When the farewell murmur dies,
And the parting footsteps press,
On our path a shadow lies,
On our hearts a loneliness.

But the cherished may come back,
And our vanished joy renew,
Far retrace a devious track,
With a love unchanged and true;
Starry eyes that shed their light
On the dark of long ago,
Shine more tenderly and bright,
Kindle with serener glow.

When the truest, that have been
With us in the walks of Time,
  Turning from its strife and din
To the higher life sublime,
  Leave us,—though we lonely grope
In this weary world behind,—
  Still we trust the larger hope
With our better being twined.

  But when friends — or counted such,
Linked with many a tender tie,
  Souls we worshiped overmuch,
With an homage pure and high,—
  Those we thought of kith and kin
In the realms of mind and heart,
  Still to be, as they had been,
Of our very life a part;—

  Oh, to see them day by day
Lose that magic power to bless!
  Oh, to feel them wear away —
Feel that nearness growing less!
  Is there art to heal the pain,
Bring the aching heart relief,
  When with anguish wild and vain
Deepens down this deepest grief?

A COMPLAINT.

Sweet bird that chants so joyous strain,
   Wake glad your early songs and late;
Pour free your jubilant heart amain,
   The live long day—who needst but wait
The twilight hush, to seek again
                 Your nest and mate.

And ye that grosser instincts bear,
   That roam the homeless wilderness;
Whom nature haunts with hungry care,
   Or fiercest brutal passions press;
Ye too may turn to love-built lair,
                 And cubs' caress.

And ye that pipe, with droning shrill,
   From shrub, and tree, your vesper sigh,—
Ye lowly insect tribes that fill
   The gloom with night-long minstrelsy,
Blow wide your homely reeds that trill
                 Love's lullaby.

And ye that prone in darkness keep,
  Whose life but earthy senses bind,—
Ye nameless reptile brood that creep
  Low on the outer verge of mind,
Ye too may own companionship,
              And love of kind.

Earth, wandering, bears a tranquil breast,
  Content a kindred orb to own;
With stars that constellated rest,
  The ether's purple deeps are sown;
All things the law of Love attest,
              Save Man alone!

Life's riddles dark—ah me!—are vain,
  All vain, these beauty-dreams that haunt?
While from the worm we dare disdain,
  Comes up Love's roundelay to taunt
Our empty breasts' wild, yearning pain,
              And deathless want.

When shall our souls the joys confess,
  That to the lowliest creatures come,
Their meaner lives to charm and bless?
  When shall our weary hearts that roam
So lonely and companionless,
              Find rest and home?

RE-EMERGED.

On tranquil tides afar lie isles of Summer,
  Where shine serene, mantled in tropic calm,
    Olive, magnolia, palm;
Along whose shores the billows lapsing murmur
    Their glad immortal psalm.

Yet were these, fair, the radiant sunlight gilding,
  Out of the deeps where slimy creatures stray,
    Out of the briny spray,
Slowly through long uncounted years upbuilding
    Into the light of day.

So erst my heart, in seas of foregone anguish,
  Sunken too deep for plummet-line of hope,
    Striving, did faint and grope,
Ages on ages, and despairing languish,
    And with all monsters cope.

Or rising thence, through oft alternate burning
And glacier-griding as the cycles run.
Or fiercer strife anon
Of earthquake shock, yearned with a deathless yearning
Toward love's transcendent sun;

And ever of some fateful force the urgence
Confessed, like all things fair that upward grow
Out of the dark below,
The admonition of a fair emergence,
And of the morning glow;

The vision of a bright supernal yonder,
Of verdured vales with harvest fields along,
Where happy gleaners throng;
Of flowery groves where spicy breezes wander,
And jubilant with song.

At length through thee, O Friend—O Spirit tender!
O best beloved!—out of the years forlorn
My darkened soul is born—
Out of the deeps, into the sapphire splendor
Of a transcendent morn.

27

Lit with the light divine, there lies a glory
    On all the land, enrobed in living green —
        Love's radiant glow and sheen;
More marvellous the zephyr's whispered story
        Of beauty yet unseen.

While all day long the billows' lips are pressing
    The golden sands, with new - world splendors bright:
        Kisses that may requite
Love infinite — repay the priceless blessing,
        Precious, of life and light.

And oh! more fair than crowned the Summers olden,
    Along the hills, late lifted from the brine,
        Shall fragrant garlands twine;
In Autumn suns all luscious fruits hang golden,
        And purple clusters shine.

CENTENNIAL.

Turn backward—turn the horoscope of Time
Backward a hundred years,
O year sublime!
Lo! by the sea,
Anxious and bowed in tears,
Tearful but not forlorn,
Columbia sitting by the cradled form
Of one but newly born;
Sitting with mother-breast all full and warm,
Feeding thy infant life, O Liberty!

Now in her matron pride she sees thee stand
Unto full stature grown;
From strand to strand,
Wide leagues away—
Still on—and all thine own,
Stretches thy fair estate;
From Isles of Palm to belts of Northern pine,
From where the Golden Gate
Looks on the sea, to the Atlantic brine;
Transfigured all in the new-risen day!

A hundred years! O who so wise to know
        The good thy years have brought.—
        To rightly show
        What work divine
Our hands through thee have wrought?
By thee inspired to toil
We builded—building better than we planned;
        Though shaped in grime and moil,
Before our thought embodied full and grand,
We stand abashed,—knowing the work is thine.

To-day thy Commerce spreads her snowy sail
        On the remotest main;
        And many a vale
        Where wakes the sound
Of forge and loom and plane,
        Where Learning builds her shrine,
Faith lights her altars, Art her temple rears,
        Where homes fond hearts entwine,
Where harvests yield their wealth of golden ears;
Was at thy birth a wilderness profound.

Through mountain reach,by hill and moor and mead
        We stretch the iron way,
        On which the steed
        That never tires,
Treads with exultant neigh;

The plowman turning o'er
The farthest glebe, a joyful tremor feels;
The woodman from his door
Hears from afar the sound of rolling wheels;—
Hearing, his soul with nobler impulse fires.

And here to-day, where thou didst wake to birth—
Life from the Life Divine!
Owning thy worth,
A mighty throng
Come—pilgrims to thy shrine,
Than armed host more grand!
Never before such sound of hurrying feet
Was heard in all the land;
And still they come,—bearing an homage meet;
And still,—and twice a hundred thousand strong!

And hither from across the stormy main
Have the far Nations brought,
And not in vain,
To honor thee,
Works that their hands have wrought;
Treasures of every zone:
Fur of all beasts that tread the Polar snow;
Sheaves from all harvests sown;
Gems, spices, gums—all plants, all fruits that grow
In gardens cradled on the Tropic sea.

And dearer than all wealth, or proud device
From Labor's tireless hand,
Bought with the price
Of precious blood—
Freedom in all the land!
Lighting the hills of Time,
Onward the morning glow of Freedom runs,—
Onward from clime to clime;
Lo! Afric's sons reaching to Afric's sons
A helping hand across the briny flood!

And though the evil Hosts that round thee stood
On that momentous day
Of Motherhood,
That gave thee life,
Dare still thy children slay;
-Aye!—Though must be again,
And yet again, thy battle fought and won.—
Must be thy patriots slain,
O Liberty! as they of Lexington,
And they that fell in Gettysburg's wild strife;—

Though too—O shame!—thy sons against thee turn
Schooled in all low desires;
With hearts that burn
With greed of gold,
Or lusts that power inspires;

Yet will we not despair:
The God of Nations shall all gods dethrone,
All realms dissolve in air,
Save that wherein each soul shall have its own,—
The Key to its own destiny shall hold.

We hark the chimes that ring thy natal year:
A far-off minstrelsy
We seem to hear;
And sweeter than
The bells' "Sweet bye and bye,"
Is the low-heard refrain;
A music that our ears have waited long,
Erewhile to swell amain;
The prelude to the glad millennial song
Of—"Peace on earth; peace and good will to Man."

ASPIRATION.

My heart's aspiring is, to me,
Of every good the prophecy—
The seed-corn of the time to be;
 And though I mourn its planting vain
 Till dewy tears, like summer rain,
 Have freely watered all the plain,
Erewhile my gladdened eyes shall dwell
On sheaves of plenty, ripened well,
 Nor be my toil in vain.

Though stubborn glebe be loth to yield,
Though only wrought to fallow field
By pointed share, oft newly-steeled;
 Though late the tender blade appears,
 Though slow the fruitful stalk uprears,
 And long ere, glad, the well-filled ears
I crib;—the harvest's ample store
Shall safely garnered be before
 The winter storm appears.

So will I trust;—in faith and prayer
Plant truth and friendship everywhere;
And love, O seed of harvests rare!
    Deep in some gentle bosom warm
    That thrills, as mine, in calm and storm,
    To beauty's glance and glowing form;
Nor doubt the Autumn days shall shine,
Full-crowned and rich in corn and wine—
   · True hearts, fond, full and warm.

For this I hold:—however crossed
By drouth or flood, by storm or frost,
No stroke of honest toil is lost;
    That still one purpose holds through all,
    Whatever evil fate befall,
    That unto each, or great or small,
Or soon or late is justice done
In every land beneath the sun;—
    That God is over all.

28

WEDDED LOVE.

In the blue that bends above us,
  Shining far,
Never alien star that mated
  Alien star;
Though with light the purple ether
  Depths are sown,
Every orb there steadfast burneth—
  Faithful turning to ITS OWN.

Like as they, are we, fate-chosen—
  Mine and thine;
So thy heart, O true heart! wedded
  Unto mine,
Like two flowers that grow together
  In the grove,
With one root, one stem, one fragrance,
  And one sun—the sun of Love.

FORTY YEARS AGO.

To-day the paths my infant footsteps pressed,
    I tread, in stranger guise;
I climb the hills, whose woodland-mantled crest
    First met my infant eyes;
On grassy mound, in Autumn's paling glow,
    I sit and muse, where in the olden time
I sat and dreamed—dreams only Youth may know
        Oh! dreams sublime,
    Dreamed forty years ago.

The pines above me sing as erst they sung:
    The well-remembered lyre
I hear again, but not the Prophet-tongue—
    " Aspire, O Heart ! aspire ;"
As from some prisoned Ariel's lips of woe,
    The voice wherein their murmurous boughs complain ;
Far off I hear, in accents faint and low,
        The sad refrain
    Of—" Forty years ago."

How much I miss that Memory's pictures hold:
     Now but a tiny rill
The brook whereon at springtime-flood of old
     I built the mimic mill;
Up to the spring, whence its pure waters flow,
  I wend, and from its shrunken tide partake;
Oh! but for once the keener thirst to know
     Its wave did slake,
     Slake—forty years ago.

Where stretched the moor that foretime seemed to mock
     At Labor's hand benign,
In pastures green now roam the bleating flock,
     Wide graze the lowing kine;
Where Autumn woods erewhile did flame and glow,
  Outspreads a furrowed field, all bare and brown;
How oft I shook for eager hands below,
     The ripe nuts down,
     There—forty years ago!

Once more I roam where oft with dog and gun
     I scoured the wooded glen;
Oft set the snare upon the rabbit's run,
     Or by the woodchuck's den;

Let him who will, hunt elk and buffalo,
  With fearless aim bring down the moose and bear;
No sport the hunter of the wild may know,
      Than this more rare—
    Of forty years ago.   :

Again beneath the orchard trees I stray,
    The trees I used to climb;
But oh! somehow the apples lack to-day
    The flavor of old time;
Though still their shining globes lie thick below—
  In blushing heaps, green, red, and gold, I see ;
Is it, this change—alas! I hardly know—
      In them or me,
    Since forty years ago?

The spot where stood the home that gave me birth,
    With grass is overgrown;
Alone is left of all that ample hearth
    One solitary stone.
Ah! since that day, though I have wandered so,
  Have seen remotest firesides blaze and shine,
None have I found to match that warmth and glow,
      That beam divine
    Of forty years ago.

Still stands, as then, the school-house old; renewed,
  And old again; to me
The same as when upon its benches rude
  I conned my A B C;
Still carvings quaint the desk and lintels show,—
 The work of hands beyond their task's employ;
If but by this, the boy to-day, I know
   Is as the boy
  Of forty years ago.

What nameless sins through ferule's sting and smart
  Did I there expiate;
Some unrepented still—obdurate heart!
  Now I recall—so late—
The schoolmate maiden that did tempt me so;
 Yet I forgave her all:—and it were bliss,
At thrice its price of stripes, thy sweets to know,
   O stolen kiss
  Of forty years ago!

Last night I sat beside that saucy maid,
  The same, yet not the same;
The frosts of Time had touched each auburn braid,
  But left her heart, her name;

From childhood's years had it been ours to grow,
    As we together grew—I questioned Fáte,—
Would she, unwedded, still have waited so,
        My gentle mate
        Of forty years ago?

To know what might have been, why should I seek?—
        The good that may not be;
The Sibyl better silence keep than speak
        Too late for Destiny;
Yet had it been my lot such joy to know,—
    O foolish Heart ! what wayward pulse is thine ;
For all our dreams, it may be better so,
        O schoolmate mine
        Of forty years ago!

The Comrades of old days—oh! where are they?
        Far from their native soil,
Unto what lands gone each his separate way,—
        Into what fields of toil?
Some cherished names the marble tablets show,
    And some, alas! are fallen more than they;
Some toward a nobler manhood strive and grow
        Still, day by day,
        As forty years ago.

And where, the forms more comely in my eyes,—
 That more in beauty grew,
Their faces lit with Learning's morning-rise,
 And with a purpose new?
By Pleasure some, some lured by Fashion's show,
 Some, crowned with Woman's fairest crown to-day,
Have sown the world with men;—as erst did sow
 Our mothers,—they
  Of forty years ago.

The vision fades,—the scenes of Childhood fly,—
 Recedes the Primal Age;
Upon my pen the sunset-shadows lie,
 My tears despoil the page;
And I full soon, the waiting fields to sow
 For harvests new, afar again shall roam;
Once more adieu—the last—I bid thee, O
 My Boyhood's Home
  Of forty years ago!

O Heart of Youth! O Soul of Prophecy!
 Go with me on my way;
Fore-herald still more happy days to be,
 That evermore delay;

For oh! not all in vain the dreams that so
  Have led my weary feet by crystal streams;
Though some have fled,—thank God! some wax and grow
      To fairer dreams
    Than forty years ago.

And may I, free from Time's decay and rust,
    Still keep Youth's horoscope;
Keep all undimmed my childhood's love and trust,
    My childhood's faith and hope;
That at the last, when fades Earth's fleeting show,—
  Falls round my life the twilight's gathering haze,
A bright Beyond shall beckon, shine and glow,
    As in the days
    Of forty years ago.

TO A WATER-LILY.

O LILY ! that dost sit with queenly brow,
Lapped on the tranquil wave in regal bloom,
  The fairest, thou
Of all the hosts whose beauty lights the gloom
 Of leafy haunts, where no rude step intrudes;
Your nectared sweets intense afar perfume
  The wildwood solitudes.

Thou hadst thy birth in some ecstatic hour
Of Nature's youthful passion undefiled;
  O peerless flower !
By many a reedy tarn, her dearest child
 The mother-breast still nurtures, warm and true:
And taught are all the creatures of the wild
  To yield their homage due.

The Sun-fish watching by her unhatched spawn,
Oft turns to gaze upon thy wondrous show;
　　The gentle Fawn
That slakes his noontide thirst, as wading slow
　The limpid pool, thy slender stem beside,
Bends wistful on thy diadem of snow
　　His wild eyes, wonder-wide.

The Bobolink, whose joyous carol thrills
With music rare the woodlands far away,
　　One moment stills
His matin song to look on thee, and pay
　Obeisance low, and then more glad and free
Exultant pours, in raptured roundelay,
　　His loyal heart to thee.

The Waves with gentle arms do thee enfold,
With soft caress their love for thee declare;
　　As half untold,
They round thee linger, press thy bosom fair;
　Then pass the tranquil mere's full-brimming urn,
Afar the river's rocky channel dare—
　　The waiting mill-wheel turn.

With passion pure the Zephyr stoops to kiss
Thy dewy lips till faint with ecstacy;
         Or drunk with bliss
That in fond heart aspires, he wanders free,
   Anon low whispers to the listening grove,
In mystic tongue, his lavish praise of thee,—
      A lover's tale of love.

   In thee there dwells a chastened spirit fine,
That in all matchless grace doth thee array ;
         What art divine
In waxy leaf and pearly petals—yea,
   Of loveliness, what miracle sublime !
And thou didst spring out of the miry clay—
      Out of the muck and slime.

   And did there come down to thy prisoned heart
Some dream transcendent of the days to be?
         The pain and smart
Of vain, long, weary yearning to be free?
   The premonition of a glory won,
Throned in thy splendor on the purple sea,
      With kisses of the sun?

O Lily ! In thy form do I behold
  Our being typed ? Do we, too, upward grow?
      Our life enfold,
As doth thy bud, a summer's radiant show?
  And all this sense of longing, doubt and dread—
Is it the spring-time quickening, felt below,
      Down in the mucky bed?

  Within the soul a world of beauty lies:
Out of this earthly soil of gloom and night
      We too shall rise
Erelong to realm unseen of mortal sight,
  Whereof hath poet sung and prophet told;
And in that fairer clime of love and light
      Life's perfect flower unfold.

As to her best beloved the mother's heart
Still yearns when passed is childhood's tender age, —
When from her home and hearth she bids him go,
The stay and builder of the days to be;
As unto him, while loving tears do flow,
Her blessing with the parting kiss is given,
To him that is of her own life a part,
Asking upon his head the smiles of Heaven ;
So do I yearn to thee, O lettered Page !
As hers my love — as hers my prayer for thee.

Born in a world of books, O Book of mine !
To-day, with noise-dulled ear, may pass thee by;
Born to thy destiny, albeit late,
All that to thee belong the Years shall give :
If Prophet of the Better Time we wait,
If Truth's evangel, Beauty's messenger :
If the high Art, however rude, is thine,
That can the soul to nobler impulse stir,
Serving its deeper need, thou shalt not die :
Use is the deed of life to all that live.

www.ingramcontent.com/pod-product-compliance
Lightning Source LLC
Chambersburg PA
CBHW030406270326
41926CB00009B/1297